"*Finding Exodus in America* by Broyde and Travis succeeds in bringing Exodus alive for an American audience and gives a new, relevant version of liberty for the twenty-first century. Any American concerned about the country's future will enjoy and benefit."

—GIDON ROTHSTEIN,
author of *Murderer in the Mikdash*

"Rabbis Broyde and Travis put forward the idea that the Exodus influenced the founders of the American Republic and their belief that freedom can only be preserved by a strong legal system. In showing us how the Biblical story delivers that message, they show that the Exodus is not simply a story of Jewish liberation but a guide for the world in how to create a society that both values and can sustain individual freedom."

—IRA BEDZOW,
Emory University

Finding America
in Exodus

FINDING AMERICA
in EXODUS

A Blueprint for "A More Perfect Union"
in the 21st Century

Michael J. Broyde
and Reuven Travis

WIPF & STOCK · Eugene, Oregon

FINDING AMERICA IN EXODUS
A Blueprint for "A More Perfect Union" in the 21st Century

Wipf & Stock
An Imprint of Wipf and Stock Publishers
199 W. 8th Ave., Suite 3
Eugene, OR 97401

www.wipfandstock.com

PAPERBACK ISBN: 978-1-6667-4899-4
HARDCOVER ISBN: 978-1-6667-4900-7
EBOOK ISBN: 978-1-6667-4901-4

SEPTEMBER 22, 2022 1:23 PM

In honor of our dear friend and colleague
RABBI DR. DON SEEMAN

in recognition of his passion, perseverance,
and commitment to building and sustaining
The New Toco Shul

The German poet Heinrich Heine wrote, "Since the Exodus, freedom has always spoken with a Hebrew accent." Since 1776, freedom has also spoken with an American accent in many places.

BRUCE FEILER
*AMERICA'S PROPHET: HOW THE STORY
OF MOSES SHAPED AMERICA*

Contents

Acknowledgements

T OGETHER WE WISH TO thank Emory University's Center for the Study of Law and Religion for their help with this volume as well as Ariel Liberman, who is currently pursuing his doctorate in law at Emory, for his excellent help in proofing and editing our final manuscript.

We are also indebted to Sefaria (www.sefaria.org), a nonprofit organization that, in its own words, is dedicated to assembling "a free, living library of Jewish texts." All translations of biblical verses in this book are taken from *Tanakh: A New Translation of the Holy Scriptures according to the Traditional Hebrew Text* which appears on its website unless otherwise indicated.[1] Thanks to Sefaria, this translation is available in the public domain with a free public license.

Individually, Rabbi Broyde would like to thank his extended family who have regularly discussed matters of biblical interpretation with him. He wouldl like to thank his wife Channah and his children Joshua, Aaron, Rachel, and Deborah who have each contributed to his understanding of Torah. Similarly, he would like to thank Joshua's wife Suzanne, and Rachel's husband Orr, each of whom has contributed in too many ways to count.

Rabbi Travis thanks his wife Laura for always helping him carve out the space he needs to pursue his passions, whether those be teaching or writing. Without her support, this book would have never come to be.

1. *Tanakh: A New Translation of the Holy Scriptures according to the Traditional Hebrew Text.*

About the Authors

MICHAEL J. BROYDE

Rabbi Broyde is Professor of Law at Emory University School of Law and a Senior Fellow at the Center for the Study of Law and Religion at Emory University. His primary areas of interest are law and religion, Jewish law and ethics, and comparative religious law. In addition to Jewish law and family law, Rabbi Broyde has taught Federal Courts, Alternative Dispute Resolution, and Secured Credit and Bankruptcy. He received his *juris doctor* degree from New York University and his published note appears in the law review. Following law school, he clerked for Judge Leonard I. Garth of the United States Court of Appeals for the Third Circuit. In 2018, Rabbi Broyde won a Fulbright Senior Scholar Fellowship to study religious arbitration in diverse western democracies.

Rabbi Broyde was ordained (יורה יורה ידין ידין) as a rabbi by Yeshiva University and was a member (דין) of the Beth Din of America, the largest Jewish law court in America. He served as director of that court during the 1997–1998 academic year while on leave from Emory. Rabbi Broyde was also the founding rabbi of the Young Israel synagogue in Atlanta, a founder of the Atlanta Torah MiTzion Kollel study program, and a board member of many organizations in Atlanta.

REUVEN TRAVIS

Prior to his career as an educator, Rabbi Travis spent fifteen years as a consultant, as well as an advertising and marketing executive. There, he worked for large Fortune 500 firms such as Georgia-Pacific and Ogilvy & Mather. He developed strategic business and marketing plans for a variety of consumer-packaged goods and financial services companies. He then changed professions and started his career as an educator. In this role, he has taught a wide range of classes, including courses on Jewish law, Bible, Jewish history, Zionism, the Shoah, Israel advocacy, American history and civics, and African American history.

Rabbi Travis earned his bachelor's degree from Dartmouth College, where he graduated Phi Beta Kappa, with a double major in French literature and political science. He holds an additional master's degree in teaching from Mercer University and earned a master's in Judaic studies from Spertus College. He received his rabbinic ordination in 2006 from Rabbi Michael J. Broyde, dean of the Atlanta Torah MiTzion Kollel, after spending four years studying with Rabbi Broyde and members of the kollel.

In addition to his collaboration with Rabbi Broyde on the book of Genesis, *Sex in the Garden: Consensual Encounters Gone Bad,* Rabbi Travis has published three scholarly works. These works looked at the book of Job, the book of Numbers, and the book of Genesis, respectively. He also authored a series of books about the weekly parasha for parents and educators of children in the third, fourth, and fifth grades.

This volume is the second of five expected volumes (a commentary on the Torah for contemporary America) that we hope to produce.

CHAPTER ONE

The Influence of Exodus
on America's Founders

I T CAN BE QUITE difficult to retell a well-known story, especially if the purpose of the retelling is to counter people's common understanding of the story. This was the core challenge we faced when embarking on this book. The Exodus story is known not only to Jews, but to people of all faiths and nationalities. Ask any-one to describe the central themes of Exodus, and they will likely answer, "freedom." We don't disagree but reading Exodus solely as a tale of liberation and freedom misses the ultimate lesson the Torah wished to convey with this enduring saga. It also misses what Americans can learn from Exodus.

America's founders were, as we will soon discuss, intimately aware of the Exodus narrative. And this leads us to ask a question that underlies this book: what, if any, affect did the Exodus story have on the founder's vision for the society they hoped to craft after breaking free from Great Britain?

To answer this question, we will, in the next chapter, consider the various lessons America's founders could have gleaned from Exodus. You might ask, why even propose that America's found-ing has roots in the Exodus story? The answer is quite simple. The earliest of the English settlers to arrive in the New World, the men and women who founded Jamestown in 1607, likened themselves to Moses and the Israelites who fled Egypt.[1] More telling is the Pilgrims, who set sail on the Mayflower in September 1620 in search of a place in which they could practice their religion free of persecution. It is well established that they saw themselves as the New Israelites, reliving the Exodus saga. Bruce Feiler, the author of *America's Prophet: How the Story of Moses Shaped America*, described the Pilgrims' mindset as:

> Everything the Pilgrims had done for two decades was designed to fulfill their dream of creating God's New Israel. When they first left England for Holland in 1608, they described themselves as the chosen people, casting off the yoke of their pharaoh, King James. A dozen years later, when they embarked on a grander exodus, to America, their leader, William Bradford, proclaimed their mission to be as vital as that of "Moses and the Israelites when they went out of Egypt." And when, after sixty-six days on the Atlantic, they finally arrived at Cape Cod, they were brought to their knees in gratitude for safe passage through their own Red Sea.[2]

In a very real sense, the Pilgrims thought of their lives and experiences as literal reenactments of the biblical drama set forth in the book of Exodus. To put it differently, the Pilgrims "saw themselves as the children of Israel; America was their Promised Land; the Atlantic Ocean their Red Sea; the Kings of England were the Egyptian pharaohs; the American Indians the Canaanites."[3]

This perspective did not end with the early settlers of America. It was also present in the thoughts and writings of America's founders. For instance, during the American Revolution, Thomas Paine's *Common Sense*, published in January 1776, had a profound impact on the colonists and helped inflame their desire for independence. There, Paine described King George III as the "sullen tempered pharaoh of England." Perhaps the most famous example of the influence of Exodus on America's early leaders is a letter

1. Bruce Feiler, *America's Prophet*, 8.
2. Feiler, *America's Prophet*, 8.
3. Freund, "How the Exodus Story Created America."

sent by George Washington after his election to the presidency to the members of Congregation Mickve Israel in Savanah, Georgia[4]:

> May the same wonder-working Deity, who long since delivered the Hebrews from their Egyptian oppressors, planted them in the promised land, whose providential agency has lately been conspicuous in establishing these United States as an independent nation, still continue to water them with the dews of heaven.[5]

Given this, it is reasonable to conclude that the American founders' thoughts and decisions, be it consciously or unconsciously, were influenced by the Exodus story. Let us now delve into Exodus to identify what those influences might have been.

4. Congregation Mickve Israel is one of the oldest synagogues in the United States. It was established in 1735 by a group of mostly Sephardic Jewish immigrants of Spanish-Portuguese extraction who arrived in the new colony of Georgia from London in 1733.

5. Feiler, 4.

CHAPTER TWO

Lessons the Founders Could Have Gleaned from Exodus

A T THE PASSOVER SEDER, Jews around the world ask, "why is this night different from all other nights?" We wish to paraphrase that question and ask, "why is this book different from all other books that examine the Jews' exodus from Egypt?" Quite simply, we believe that Exodus is about more than liberation and freedom. It ought to be read as of tale full of important political lessons; indeed, this is likely how America's founders read it. Each of these lessons becomes apparent with a close reading of the Biblical text.

Liberation

Before we discuss the Jews' need for liberation, let's consider how the Jews found themselves in such a predicament.

> The Jews (who are referred to as "Hebrews" in the text) were initially welcomed to Egypt with great fanfare. Joseph had saved the country from devastating famine, and, when his brothers and father arrived in Egypt, they were warmly welcomed by Pharaoh. Genesis reads: "Then Pharaoh said to Joseph, 'As regards your father and your brothers who have come to you, the land of

> Egypt is open before you: settle your father and your
> brothers in the best part of the land; let them stay in the
> region of Goshen. And if you know some men of ability
> among them, put them in charge of my livestock."[1]

Yet, even in Joseph's lifetime, relations began to sour. Joseph, who during the famine years was second only to Pharaoh and had unfettered access to him, was distanced in the royal court by the time of his father Jacob's death. In seeking permission to return to Canaan to bury his father, Joseph is not allowed to speak directly to Pharaoh. Instead, he must make his request to the royal court, as the verse says, "Do me this favor, and lay this appeal before Pharaoh."[2]

After the deaths of Joseph and his twelve brothers, the situation deteriorates quickly; however, the Jews seem oblivious to this at first. Indeed, life was good for the Jews in Egypt: "the Israelites were fertile and prolific; they multiplied and increased very greatly, so that the land was filled with them."[3] Nevertheless, the Jews apparent prosperity was a cause for great consternation among Pharaoh and his advisers. "And he [Pharaoh] said to his people," reads Exodus, "'Look, the Israelite people are much too numerous for us. Let us deal shrewdly with them, so that they may not increase; otherwise in the event of war they may join our enemies in fighting against us and rise from the ground.'"[4]

While the text is silent on the details of this "shrewd" plan, the Jewish oral tradition has much to say about it.[5] The starting point for this oral exposition is the unusual Biblical term characterizing Pharaoh's enslavement of the Israelites— פרך (*farech*)—a term used only this once in the Bible (and whose etymology is unclear). The word is usually translated as "harsh" or "ruthless," as in "the Egyptians ruthlessly (בְּפָרֶךְ) imposed upon the Israelites the

---

1. Genesis 47:5–6.
2. Genesis 50:4.
3. Exodus 1:7.
4. Exodus 1:9–10.
5. Tanhuma, Beha'alotcha 13.

various labors that they made them perform."[6] The sages suggest that this uncommon word is actually a compound of two other words: פה (*peh* or mouth) and רך (*rach* or smooth). This teaches us that Pharaoh's enslavement of the Jews was achieved using his "*peh rach*"—his suave demeanor.

The story continues.

Pharaoh announces a national plan to build upon Egypt's infrastructure and initially takes part in the effort. He even picks up tools to work and asks the Jews to join him (presumably to show that they are loyal citizens). However, the next day, after having established the Jews as motivated volunteers, Pharaoh and the other Egyptians cease their participation. They are replaced by taskmasters who are charged with overseeing the Jews' labor. What was at first a voluntary work force was suddenly and quickly changed to one of servitude. As one author put it, "Pharaoh lulled the Israelites into a slavery that seized upon the spirit of human kindness and motivated interest and then abruptly quashed the human agency and free expression in pursuit of mechanizing a 'quota of bricks.'"[7]

Work conditions for the now enslaved Jews were quite harsh. "The Egyptians ruthlessly imposed upon the Israelites the various labors that they made them perform. Ruthlessly they made life bitter for them with harsh labor at mortar and bricks and with all sorts of tasks in the field."[8]

This would only get worse.

"The king of Egypt spoke to the Hebrew midwives, one of whom was named Shiphrah and the other Puah, saying, 'When you deliver the Hebrew women, look at the birthstool, if it is a boy, kill him; if it is a girl, let her live.'"[9] Such inhumane conditions took their toll on the Jews. They reached a breaking point, as the verse states: "The Israelites were groaning under the bondage and cried out; and their cry for help from the bondage rose up to God."[10]

6. Exodus 1:13–14.

7. Ilana Fodiman-Silverman, "Salvation from servitude."

8. Exodus 1:13–14.

9. Exodus 1:15–16.

10. Exodus 2:23.

To be clear, it is not just slavery that drives the Jews to despair, as we see from another critical point in Jewish history. Centuries after the events of Exodus, when the Jews faced genocide due to wicked Haman's scheming, Queen Esther (whose identity as a Jew was unknown to both Haman and the king) appeals to King Ahasuerus to save her people. Consider how she phrases her plea: She says, "For we have been sold, my people and I, to be destroyed, massacred, and exterminated. **Had we only been sold as bondmen and bondwomen,** I would have kept silent; for the adversary is not worthy of the king's trouble."[11] [emphasis added] The Jewish people can apparently withstand harsh oppression and even slavery, but tossing babies into the Nile to exterminate them is more than the Jews (or any people) can endure.

The stage is thus set for liberation.

In this model, liberation is the end of slavery—the end of the Jews' suffering. Nothing more. Without saying this directly, the rabbis hint at this in one of the central rituals of the Passover seder, the Dayenu prayer. Consider its opening lyrics.

> *Verse 1:*
> If He had brought us out from Egypt, and had not carried out judgments against them
> — Dayenu, it would have sufficed!
> *Verse 2:*
> If He had carried out judgments against them, and not against their idols
> — Dayenu, it would have sufficed!
> *Verse 3:*
> If He had destroyed their idols, and had not smitten their first-born
> — Dayenu, it would have sufficed!
> *Verse 4:*
> If He had smitten their first-born, and had not given us their wealth
> — Dayenu, it would have sufficed!

Freedom in this approach implies freedom from slavery which implies liberation. Where does an exodus fit into this

11. Esther 7:4.

scheme? The Greeks saw liberation as the central theme of the book of Exodus, and most modern readers would likely agree. Indeed, by the arrival of the sixth plague, liberation is inevitable.[12] However, inevitable does not mean that this is the only way to read the story, and an exodus is not the only hypothetical outcome.

Let us move on to the next approach.

Freedom and Citizenship

An alternative reading of the Exodus story is that freedom ought to be tied to citizenship. Once again, a close examination of the text supports this.

For example, when Moses first appears before Pharaoh, he seems deceptive in his request of the Egyptian ruler, saying, "The God of the Hebrews has become manifest to us. Let us go, we pray, a distance of three days into the wilderness to sacrifice to our God, lest [God] strike us with pestilence or sword,"[13] An odd comment if exodus is the ultimate goal.[14] Pharaoh not only refuses Moses,

---

12. In its account of the first five plagues, the Torah describes Pharaoh's refusal to send out the enslaved Jews with words such as: "And Pharaoh's heart was hardened." Beginning with the plague of boils, the sixth of the ten plagues, the wording changes: "**And the Lord hardened** the heart of Pharaoh." This change remains in place in the description of each of the final plagues. In commenting on this linguistic change, Nachmanides, one of the most renowned medieval Biblical commentators, explains the phrase "Pharaoh's heart was hardened" to mean that it is Pharaoh who is obstinate. It is Pharaoh who is oblivious to the impact of the first five plagues. However, by the sixth plague, Pharaoh finally "gets it." He understands that liberation is inevitable. God therefore hardens Pharaoh's heart so that he will stick to his refusal to free the Jews. This, says Nachmanides, does not deprive Pharaoh of his free will. Rather, it allows him to be true to his first and instinctual choice not to free the Jews.

13. Exodus 5:3.

14. There are some who claim that Moses was not deceitful at all, but rather that his was a genuine request meant to serve as a test for Pharaoh. If Pharaoh refused even this minor request, his hard-heartedness and stubbornness would be revealed to all. If, however, he would have acceded to this request, the Jews would indeed have returned to Egypt after several days, and Moses would then have continued to negotiate slowly for their freedom. For

but he also makes life more difficult for the Jews. He instructs his taskmasters, "You shall no longer provide the people with straw for making bricks as heretofore; let them go and gather straw for themselves. But impose upon them the same quota of bricks as they have been making heretofore; do not reduce it, for they are shirkers; that is why they cry, 'Let us go and sacrifice to our God!'"[15]

By the third plague (lice), Pharaoh's resolve seems to be weakening. He proposes to Moses that the Jews "go and sacrifice to your God within the land."[16] Moses, of course, rejects this compromise. Pharaoh then makes a counteroffer: "I will let you go to sacrifice to your God in the wilderness; but do not go very far. Plead, then, for me."[17] This, too, Moses rejects, and the plagues continue.

After the ninth plague (darkness), Pharaoh's resolve is even weaker. He offers yet another compromise: "Go, worship God! Only your flocks and your herds shall be left behind; even your dependents may go with you."[18]

What is implicit in this new, revised offer? It is that Pharaoh now sees an alternative to liberation. The Jews will not leave Egypt. They will be freed to become Egyptian citizens. It is as if Pharaoh is saying to Moses, go, but return, and we will together build a new bi-cultural nation, one in which we can all worship freely.

Could this work? Possibly. The Jews had been living in Egypt for centuries, and there were some, according to the Jewish oral tradition, who had Egyptian patrons, along with wealth and honor. These individuals enjoyed the life they had in Egypt and did not want to leave.[19] Remember, too, that their leader Moses grew up as royalty in Pharaoh's household, which means he would have had

---

a deeper discussion of this topic, see "Moshe's Deceit in his Negotiations with Pharaoh" by Rav Elchanan Samet, https://www.etzion.org.il/en/tanakh/torah/sefer-shemot/parashat-bo/bo-moshes-deceit-his-negotiations-pharaoh.

15. Exodus 5:7–8.

16. Exodus 5:21.

17. Exodus 5:24.

18. Exodus 10:24.

19. It must be noted that the sages saw such individuals as sinners.

the knowledge and connections to pull off structuring this new society.

For their part, the Egyptians themselves seemingly bought into this idea. Why else would they lend "objects of silver and gold, and clothing" to the Jews as they were leaving Egypt after the tenth and final plague.[20] Why would the Egyptians be "favorably disposed" towards the Jews if they did not expect them to return?[21]

Those of us that live in the United States and know post-Civil War American history understand the challenges and limitations related to attempted integration of recently freed slaves into society as full citizens. We struggle with this to this very day. This, however, does not negate the possibility of reading the Exodus story as one emphasizing freedom as being tied to citizenship.

We will soon see that God himself is fiercely opposed to this model (and therefore this reading of Exodus), but before we get there, we ought to consider yet another alternative understanding of freedom.

Revolution

The history of the antebellum South provides some context for comprehending the situation in biblical Egypt vis-à-vis its Hebrew slaves. Let's start with the numbers:

In 1808, the federal government in American banned the importation of new slaves.[22] In the first census conducted after this law went into effect, Virginia—the largest of the slave states—had a white population of 551,534. The number of enslaved individuals was 392,518. According to the last pre-Civil War census (1860), Virginia's white population had almost doubled to 1,047,299, while the number of enslaved individuals only increased by

20. Exodus 12:35.

21. Exodus 12:36.

22. The Act Prohibiting Importation of Slaves of 1807 provided that no new slaves were permitted to be imported into the United States. It took effect on January 1, 1808, the earliest date permitted by the United States Constitution.

100,000 to 490,865. [23] Similar trends were evident throughout all the southern slave states. Although the number of enslaved people as a percentage of each state's total population was decreasing, the actual number of enslaved individuals continued to grow sharply, reaching over 3.9 million in 1860. By comparison, the number was about 1.1 million in 1810. [24]

Where does the Exodus narrative fit into all this?

Ironically, southern plantation owners—that is, the slave owners—used Exodus to form their respective identities and to define their purpose in America. They saw themselves as New Israel, the "Redeemer Nation." [25] As such, they believed that they were poised "to reach the pinnacle of perfection and to carry liberty and the gospel around the globe." [26]

> Yet, the enslavers understood the potential power that the book of Exodus could exert on the people they enslaved. More than understood, they feared the Exodus narrative. "English missionaries seeking to convert enslaved Africans toiling in Britain's Caribbean colonies around the beginning of the nineteenth century preached from Bibles that conveniently removed portions of the canonical text. They thought these sections, such as Exodus, the Book of Psalms, and the Book of Revelation, could instill in slaves a dangerous hope for freedom and dreams of equality." [27]

In other words, the enslavers foresaw that an unredacted Bible would be read by the enslaved masses as a text that endorses and even demands liberation. This—combined with the brutality of slavery and the even more brutal way slave rebellions were quashed—meant slave revolts were few and far between. There were some, but not many. Three of the best known were the revolts by Gabriel Prosser in Virginia in 1800, Denmark Vesey in

---

23. https://faculty.weber.edu/kmackay/statistics_on_slavery.htm.
24. Historical Statistics of the US (1970).
25. Raboteau, *A Fire in the Bones.*
26. Raboteau, *A Fire in the Bones.*
27. Zehavi, "19th-cent. Slave Bible."

Charleston, South Carolina in 1822, and Nat Turner's Slave Rebellion in Southampton County, Virginia, in 1831.

Does this have a familiar ring to it?

As we have noted, even before Pharoah enslaved the Jews, he feared them and the threat they posed (at least in his mind) to his rule. As he said to his advisors, "Look, the Israelite people are much too numerous for us. Let us deal shrewdly with them, so that they may not increase; otherwise in the event of war they may join our enemies in fighting against us and rise from the ground."[28]

Once Pharoah enslaved the Jews, he ordered his taskmasters to work the Jews relentlessly. In the aftermath of Moses's first meeting with the Egyptian ruler, Pharoah issued the following order: "Let heavier work be laid upon those involved; let them keep at it and not pay attention to deceitful promises."[29] This did not satisfy Pharoah. He thought of the Jewish slaves as "shirkers"[30] and again made their enslavement more bitter. As the verse states, "they made life bitter for them with harsh labor at mortar and bricks and with all sorts of tasks in the field."[31] He thought to work the slaves to near-death, but this, too, was not enough. He thus "charged all his people, saying, 'Every boy that is born you shall throw into the Nile, but let every girl live.'"[32]

With this command, the Jews were no longer simply enslaved: they faced genocide. Not only genocide, but ethnic cleansing, where Jewish women would marry—out of a lack of choice—Egyptian men. Whereas before they had groaned under the "bondage of slavery," now they cried out as their babies were drowned in the Nile. It is these cries that "rose up to God,"[33] and it is with these cries that they turn to God. They seemed to place their fate in His hands. But did they? Is it possible that, like Gabriel Prosser, Denmark Vesey, and Nat Turner, the Jewish slaves

28. Exodus 1:9-10.
29. Exodus 5:9.
30. Exodus 5:17.
31. Exodus 1:14.
32. Exodus 1:22.
33. Exodus 2:23.

dreamed of rebellion? One key word in the Exodus story suggests that the answer is "yes."

According to the text, "the Israelites went up *ḥamushim* out of the land of Egypt."[34] The meaning of this Hebrew word *ḥamushim* is unclear, and there are competing oral traditions regarding how it is to be understood. Both are problematic.

The first is based on the linguistic similarity between *ḥamushim* and *ḥameish*, the Hebrew word for "five." According to this view, only one out of five (*ḥameish*) Jews left Egypt during the Exodus.[35] The remaining four-fifths died during the plague of darkness. Why? Supposedly because they were unworthy of being delivered. (We should note that the oral tradition does not say why they were unworthy.) As to why these individuals needed to perish specifically during the plague of darkness, it seems that it was to keep the matter hidden from the Egyptians, for it would have been a cause of national shame for this knowledge to have been made public.

The alternative approach is based on the more common understanding—that the word *ḥamushim* means "armed." This, of course, begs the question: Why would the Jews want to or need to leave Egypt armed?

One opinion is that even though God led them out of Egypt into the wilderness via a circuitous route, the Jews were still fearful of the Philistines living in nearby cities. As a result, they took arms, as is normal for people who go out to war or who are fearful of their neighbors.

A second opinion holds that the Jews left Egypt armed in anticipation of future wars in the wilderness. Their concerns were well-founded, as they ultimately waged war against Amalek, Midian, and Sihon and Og. Had they not left Egypt armed, they would have been unprepared for those confrontations.

A third opinion suggests that the armaments were not needed for any impending or future war. Rather, the Jews left Egypt "with

---

34. Exodus 13:18.
35. Mekhilta d'Rabbi Yishmael 13:19:3.

a high hand," that is, defiantly.[36] As one Biblical commentary described it, the Jews left "With a high hand carrying their arms and not like slaves who escape from their master."[37] In other words, by leaving armed, the Jews demonstrated that they considered themselves a people redeemed from bondage—not as escaped slaves.

The common thread between these three opinions is that none of them clarify where or how the enslaved Jews obtained weapons great enough in number to potentially engage in multiple wars! (The Biblical text itself is silent on this subject.) Could it be that the Jewish slaves were scheming to make Pharoah's worst dream—a slave revolt—come true? It is certainly plausible, especially in light of the grievances later leveled against Moses in the wilderness. Complaints such as "Was it for want of graves in Egypt that you brought us to die in the wilderness?" and "What have you done to us, taking us out of Egypt?" were raised.[38]

If achieving liberation via rebellion was a plausible (and maybe even a viable) alternative to an exodus from Egypt, then what happened? If the Jews had truly armed themselves in anticipation of rebelling, then why did they choose not to do so? Did they have a change of heart due to counter arguments offered up by Moses? Were they swayed by the awesome display of power wrought by God and the ten plagues He brought down upon Egypt? Did they simply get cold feet?

The fact that the rebellion did not take place does not render it an implausible reading of the Exodus story. Indeed, the rabbinic answer might very well be that those who died during the plague of darkness were those who wanted to stay in Egypt as part of the slave rebellion. With their deaths, God makes it extraordinarily clear that He did not want the Jews to become Egyptians.

36. Exodus 14:8.
37. See Ibn Ezra on Exodus 14:8.
38. Exodus 14:13.

Knowledge of God

We have thus far considered two alternative readings of Exodus in which the Jews could have been liberated without leaving Egypt. These alternatives were rejected by God Himself, as we will now discuss, and His rejection is premised on two important insights that can be gleaned from the Exodus narrative.

The first involves the knowledge of God.

One need not be fully versed with the Exodus narrative to have heard of the ten plagues. Even those with a cursory understanding of the story recognize that the plagues were meant to bring about the liberation of Jewish slaves and to punish Pharoah and his people for their harsh treatment of the Jews. While this is view is not wrong, it does overlook one critical element of the plagues. Discovering this element requires a bit of background knowledge about the plagues themselves.

The consensus among the Talmudic sages and later biblical commentators is that the plagues can be sorted into three groups.[39] The groupings, however, are not germane to our discussion. What interests us is the language Moses uses to introduce each set of plagues, that is, the Hebrew word *teidah*, "you shall know."

In his first encounter with Moses, Pharoah denies the very existence of God, telling Moses: "Who is God that I should heed him and let Israel go? I do not know God, nor will I let Israel go."[40] Pharoah further suggests that even if the God of the Hebrew exists, He certainly does not pay attention to the lowly creatures. (In essence, Pharoah here denies the concept of divine providence.) Finally, Pharoah takes issue with God's power, insisting that God is not able to change nature.

God responds to Pharoah's misguided arguments by word and deed. Most striking is the implied mockery of Pharoah we see

---

39. Whether the tenth plague, which killed "all the [male] first-born in the land of Egypt, from the first-born of Pharaoh who sat on the throne to the first-born of the captive who was in the dungeon, and all the first-born of the cattle," is part of this group or stands alone is a much-debated topic among biblical commentators.

40. Exodus 2:5.

in the text with the repeated use of *teidah,* "you shall know." In other words, the ruler who claimed not to know God will certainly know Him once the plagues have decimated Egypt.

Let's take a closer look at the text itself.

In response to Pharoah's claim that God does not exit, Moses informs Pharoah of the first plague with a rebuke from God Himself: "By this you shall know (*teidah*) that I am God."[41] Each of the first three plagues (Nile turning into blood, frogs, lice) is meant to reenforce this message.

The second grouping of plagues begins with flies, and prior to its onset, Moses tells Pharoah: "But on that day I will set apart the region of Goshen, where My people dwell, so that no swarms of insects shall be there, that you may know (*teidah*) that I God am in the midst of the land."[42] With His use of flies, God shows Pharoah that He is indeed concerned with—and can even control—the lowliest of creatures.

The final grouping of plagues, even more so than the previous six, seems supernatural. The Jewish oral tradition describes the hail that fell on Egypt as icy hailstones containing a flame that burned within each one.[43] The plague of darkness also went beyond the natural order, and the verses tell us: "Moses held out his arm toward the sky and thick darkness descended upon all the land of Egypt for three days. People could not see one another, and for three days no one could move about."[44] The oral tradition teaches that this darkness was palpable. How so? If people were standing, they could not sit, and if they were sitting, they could not stand or move about.[45] This provides context to the warning that Moses gives Pharoah before the final group of plagues unfolds:

41. Exodus 7:17.

42. Exodus 8:18.

43. This explanation stems from the very words of the verse that describes this plague: "So Moses held out his rod toward the sky, and God sent thunder and hail, and fire streamed down to the ground, as God rained down hail upon the land of Egypt" (Exodus 9:23).

44. Exodus 10:22–23.

45. Midrash Tanchuma.

"For this time I will send all My plagues upon your person, and your courtiers, and your people, in order that you may know (*teidah*) that there is none like Me in all the world."[46]

Pharoah, who once denied God's existence, is by the end of the plagues forced to admit that God does exist, that there is such a thing a divine provenance, and that God can in fact change the laws of nature. He and his people now know God, and so, too, do the Jewish people in a deeper and more profound manner. Their knowledge of and belief in God was only strengthened by the plagues.

But what does all this have to do with the Exodus itself?

Knowledge of God was not only a prerequisite for the Jews' departure from Egypt, but it also made their exodus a necessity. That one cannot know God and serve Him in a country as pagan as Egypt is imminently logical.[47] Yet, God's distain for Egypt goes beyond its pagan culture, as the Torah makes clear: "You shall not copy the practices of the land of Egypt where you dwelt."[48] Here we find no reference to idolatry. Rather, as the rabbinic tradition tells us, it is Egypt's sexual perversions that repel God. The rabbis understood the ancient Egyptians to be "addicted to carnality, in all forms of the forbidden relationships, and with males and cattle."[49]

The question then is: what is the most appropriate place to serve God? This leads us to the second reason for why God rejects

---

46. Exodus 9:14.

47. The following midrash illustrates the point. In commenting on the verse "And the Lord spoke unto Moses and Aaron in the land of Egypt, saying" (Exodus 12 :1), the midrash posits: "In the land of Egypt" implies that it was outside the city. But perhaps it means inside the city? However, since Scripture says, "Moses said unto him: 'As soon as I am gone out of the city, I will spread forth my hands unto the Lord'" (Exodus 9:29), may not the matter be argued a fortiori? If, in order to pray-an ordinary event, Moses would insist on going outside the city, how much more so would he go outside the city to receive a communication from God-an extraordinary event? And why would God speak to him only outside the city? Because the city was full of abominations and idols.

48. Leviticus 18:3.

49. Torat Kohanim, *Acharei* 9:3.

the notion of liberation without being tied to Exodus, one that centers on the land of Israel.

THE CENTRALITY OF THE LAND OF ISRAEL

With the destruction of the Second Temple by the Romans in 70 CE, Jews were forced into long-term diaspora.[50] They rebuilt their lives. They created new communities in which they restored many of their ancestors' rituals, ranging from Sabbath observance to the thrice-daily prayers services. It seemed that they had successfully reestablished their relationship with their Father in Heaven. Yet, throughout their exile, the Jews never gave up hope that the Temple and the Davidic monarchy might be restored.

Why is this so?

By their continued existence, the Jewish people have seemingly demonstrated that one can know God and serve God in almost any place (except for corrupt or immoral locales such as Egypt). This, however, is not consistent with a careful reading of Exodus, as we can clearly see in God's first interaction with Moses. God says:

> I have marked well the plight of My people in Egypt and have heeded their outcry because of their taskmasters; yes, I am mindful of their sufferings. I have come down to rescue them from the Egyptians and to bring them out of that land to a good and spacious land, a land flowing with milk and honey, the region of the Canaanites, the Hittites, the Amorites, the Perizzites, the Hivites, and the Jebusites.[51]

Here, God makes clear the special connection between the Jewish people and the land of Israel. Here, He explicitly states that Israel is the intended destination of the freed slaves, but why? What sets the land of Israel apart from all other lands?

50. The enduring nature of the Roman exile stands in contrast to the Jew's exile to Babylonia following the destruction of the First Temple, which lasted merely seventy years.

51. Exodus 3:7–8.

The Torah gives us a hint with the following description of Israel, which is found in the book of Deuteronomy. It reads, "It is a land which your God looks after, on which your God always keeps an eye, from year's beginning to year's end."[52] Most commentators understand this to mean that God is constantly and carefully examining the morals of those who dwell in this land, and that He does this because Israel is a place of intense holiness. The Jewish oral tradition is very direct when it comes to this idea: "The Land of Israel is the holiest of all lands."[53] The Talmudic rabbis use even sharper language:

> Anyone who resides in Eretz Yisrael is considered as one who has a God, and anyone who resides outside of Eretz Yisrael is considered as one who does not have a God. As it is stated: "To give to you the land of Canaan, to be your God" (Leviticus 25:38). And can it really be said that anyone who resides outside of Eretz Yisrael has no God? Rather, this comes to tell you that anyone who resides outside of Eretz Yisrael is considered as though he is engaged in idol worship.[54]

What makes the land of Israel a reservoir of such powerful holiness?

This is a question often considered in the midrashim that are central to Judaism's oral tradition. In this tradition, God desires a dwelling place in the lower realm (our world), and He thus commands the Jewish people to build him a House of God. As the verse states: "And let them make Me a sanctuary that I may dwell among them."[55] While this *mishkan*, this House of God, was first erected in the wilderness, it would ultimately become the Holy Temple built, says the midrash, on the very spot where the creation of the world began. This spot—the Land of Israel—was the center of the world, and in its center was Jerusalem. In the very center of Jerusalem, on *Har HaBayit*, the Temple Mount, sat God's holy

---

52. Deuteronomy 11:12.
53. Genesis R. 96:5.
54. Ketubot 110b.
55. Exodus 25:8.

abode, where His presence, His *Shekhinah*, was tangibly and visibly present.

This is not to suggest that God's presence was limited to Jerusalem and the Temple itself. Indeed, various midrashim seek to disabuse us of that notion.

> *In every place,* [*where I cause my name to be remembered I will come to you and bless you*] (Exod 20:24), that is, in the Temple. . . . Rabbi Eliezer b. Yaakov says: [The Lord says:] If you come to my house I will come to your house, but if you do not come to my house I will not come to your house. To the place my heart loves, there my feet lead me.
>
> From here [Exodus 20:24] they [derived and] said: Wherever ten persons assemble in a synagogue, the Shekhinah is with them, as it is said: *God stands in the congregation of God* (Ps. 82:1). And how do we know that He is also with three people holding court? It says: *Among the judges he judges* (ibid.). And how do we know that he is also with two? It is said: *Then those who feared the Lord spoke one with another,* etc. (Mal 3:16). And how do we know that he is even with one? It is said: *In every place where I cause my name to be remembered I will come to you and bless you.*[56]

We see in this midrash an important idea, namely, that even when the *Shekhinah* is most present in the Holy Temple, it is nonetheless present in the rest of the world. However, it is the intensity of God's presence in the land of Israel that infuses it with such tremendous holiness.

Importantly, the Jewish legal tradition recognizes this fact. Notably, Nachmanides describes the legal ramifications of this in a manner most apropos to our discussion. In his commentary on Numbers (33:53), he states:

> In my opinion, this [the phrase "you shall take possession of the land and settle in it"] constitutes a positive commandment (*mitzvat asseh*). He commanded them to reside in the land and take possession of it. He had

56. Mekhilta d'Rabbi Ishmael Bahodesh, 11.

given it to them, and it was not for them to disparage the inheritance of the Lord. For them therefore to contemplate **the conquest of Babylonia, Assyria, or any other country and make their home there instead** would be a violation of a Divine commandment. [emphasis added]

Is it any wonder then that God rejects the notions of either a bi-national alliance with the Egyptians or a revolution by the Hebrew slaves to seize control of Egypt?

Once we acknowledge that freedom requires communal autonomy, we must concede that autonomy for the former slaves means their own country. Yet, as God makes clear, this was to be autonomy and liberty with a purpose, as opposed to a mere release from the bonds of slavery. His charge to the Jewish people after they leave Egypt, and prior to His giving them the Torah at Mount Sinai, is that "you shall be to Me a kingdom of priests and a holy nation."[57] Given this, it is most understandable why God insists that the Jews leave Egypt for the land of Israel, the spiritual center of the world, even if it takes them forty years to arrive.

The Dimensions of Leadership

Most contemporary readers think that the Exodus story ends when the Jews leave Egypt. They thus tend to see their forty-year sojourn in the wilderness as a story unto itself. This is a plausible way to read the story, but Exodus only truly concludes when Joshua leads the Jews into Canaan and successfully directs their conquest of the land.

With this perspective in mind, we can turn to one last approach to the story, an approach that sets forth some important insights on how the Torah defines leadership. Reading through the entire story as defined above, we see that the Exodus narrative has much to say regarding who should govern as well as how that individual should govern.

57. Exodus 19:6.

Let's start with who should govern. The Torah seems to give a definitive answer to this question in the book of Deuteronomy. It reads:

> If, after you have entered the land that your God has assigned to you, and taken possession of it and settled in it, you decide, "I will set a king over me, as do all the nations about me," you shall be free to set a king over yourself, one chosen by your God. Be sure to set as king over yourself one of your own people; you must not set a foreigner over you, one who is not your kin.[58]

The Talmudic rabbis saw in these verses a clear and absolute command. It is written:

> And so would Rabbi Yehuda say: Three mitzvot were commanded to the Jewish people upon their entrance into Eretz Yisrael: [They were commanded] to establish a king for themselves, and to cut off the seed of Amalek, and to build the Chosen House [i.e., the Temple in Jerusalem].[59]

This interpretation also appears in several medieval biblical commentaries. More tellingly, this view is codified by Maimonides in his Book of Mitzvot as a positive commandment.[60]

Despite the seeming unambiguity of such statements, there was much debate among the Sages about the true meaning of these verses in Deuteronomy. At issue were questions like: must the Jews appoint a king, or may they appoint a king? Or is the appointment of the king even a good thing?

The unusual opening words of the verses—"after you have entered the land"—are what drive these questions. These words suggest that the appointment of the king is optional, not mandatory. Moreover, the phrase "and you say" presents the possibility that the Jews might say they want a king, but it does not mandate the king's appointment. "To complicate matters further, the option

---

58. Deuteronomy 17:14–15.

59. Sanhedrin 20b.

60. Maimonides, Laws of Kings, 1:1.

of appointing a king is phrased like a standard commandment: the grammatical form of 'you shall surely set,' a cognate accusative—when the direct object is the same root as the verb—is generally a way of emphasizing a command, not an option."[61]

In other words, the simple reading (*peshat*) of the verses is that the appointment of a king is optional, not required. To read the verses otherwise runs counter to the conditional clause and cannot be considered *peshat*.[62]

Considering this debate, we believe that it is instructive to examine the actions taken by the two great leaders of the Jews in the aftermath of the Exodus (Moses and Joshua) to better glean insights about which leadership model the Torah endorses.

Moses was the greatest of the prophets, as the Torah itself attests to: "Never again did there arise in Israel a prophet like Moses—whom God singled out, face to face"[63] Moses was the Jews' great teacher, so great that he is frequently referred to as *Moshe Rabbeinu*, "our teacher Moses," in Jewish literature and legal codes. In his lifetime, he was also considered a king, as the Talmud elucidates:

> King Solomon desired to attain the status of Moses. A Heavenly voice came forth and cited this verse, "There arose not a Prophet in Israel like Moses"—neither a Prophet nor a King [can emulate the status of Moses]. Others say, no other Prophet arose, but a King [like Moses] can arise.[64]

61. Dr. Rabbi Zev Farber, "Does the Torah Really Want Us to Appoint a King?"

62. Farber, "Does the Torah Really Want Us to Appoint a King?" An additional point must be made here. While the prophet Samuel ultimately appointed two kings—first Saul, and then David—doing so was not his idea. The people demanded it, as the verse states: "All the elders of Israel gathered, and came to Samuel, to Ramah...and said to him, 'Behold, you have grown old, and your sons do not walk in your ways. Now, appoint for us a king to judge us like all the nations'" (1 Samuel 8:4–5). Indeed, Samuel's reaction was far from positive, and he eventually turned the matter over to God. God responded with similar displeasure, but nonetheless told Samuel to grant them their wish.

63. Deuteronomy 34:10.

64. Rosh Hashanah 21b.

Moses lived in an era of hereditary monarchies. Indeed, the Jews spent hundreds of years as slaves to just this type of monarch. Given the norms of his times, one would have expected Moses to appoint one of his sons as the next leader—the next king so to speak—of the Jewish people. He did not. Instead, he appoints Joshua, not one of his sons, as his successor. He did so publicly to ensure that none would question Joshua's authority.[65]

Why does Moses do this?

We believe that he intuited great danger in a hereditary monarchy as a result of hearing his fellow Israelites' accounting of the Exodus, their time in the wilderness, and their distorted recollections about life in Egypt. As if to prove the point, one complaint in Exodus reads:

> If only we had died by the hand of God in the land of Egypt, when we sat by the fleshpots, when we ate our fill of bread! For you have brought us out into this wilderness to starve this whole congregation to death.[66]

Moses may have brought the Jews out of Egypt, but he was worried that some remained attached to the customs and ideas of Egypt. Even after forty years of teaching the people how not to be Egyptian,[67] he was fearful that some wished to bring Egypt with them into the Holy Land. A hereditary monarchy would have been similar to Egypt, and, to preclude this possibility, Moses goes out of his way to name Joshua, not one of his sons, as his successor.

Joshua was, of course, a very different leader than Moses. As the midrash delineates:

65. See Deuteronomy 31:7. According to the Talmudic sages, God Himself endorsed this choice and vested in Joshua absolute authority over the people. Commenting of Moses's charge to Joshua to bring the Jews "into the land that God swore to their fathers to give them," these sages read into the verse a directive from God to Joshua. It is as if God says to Joshua: "You yourself must bring the people there. Take a rod and strike the people upon their skulls if that is what is required. You have the authority from me to do so" (Sanhedrin 8a).

66. Exodus 16:3.

67. Moses specifically commands the people: "You shall not copy the practices of the land of Egypt where you dwelt" (Leviticus 18:3).

R. Judah said in the name of Rav: When Moses our teacher was about to depart for the Garden of Eden, he said to Joshua: Ask me about any matters of law about which you are in doubt. Joshua replied: My master, have I ever left you, even for as little as one hour, and gone elsewhere? Have you not in fact written of me, "His servant Joshua the son of Nun departed not out of the Tabernacle" (Exod. 33: 1 1) [where I studied Torah constantly]? At that, Joshua's mental strength grew so weak that he forgot three hundred laws and found himself in doubt concerning seven other matters of law. The people of Israel [frustrated by Joshua's confusion] were all but ready to slay him. So, the Holy One said to him: It is impossible to teach you hundred right now but go and distract the people with warfare. Hence; "And it came to pass after the death of Moses . . . Joshua commanded: . . . Prepare you victuals, for within three days ye . . . go in to possess the Land" (Josh. 1:1 and 1:10- 11).[68]

Joshua was not the teacher that his mentor was, but he was extraordinarily dedicated to leading the Jewish people to their destination. He committed his entire life to this purpose, and, in the end, conquered six nations and thirty-one kings. Said differently, Joshua "is, first and foremost, a statesman-prophet who, unlike Moses (the lawgiver-prophet) [spends] his life in political and military roles and whose forte is in the political realm."[69]

While the book that bears his name gives us no details, Joshua, as he reached the end of his life, reflected on Moses's decision to choose him as the next leader. Moses abandoned the hereditary monarchy, and now Joshua was prepared to take it one step further. **He named no successor**, and thus, the Jewish people became tribes, with no single leader.

We want to propose here a radical rationale for Joshua's decision. We believe he was driven, in part, by the notion that he, like Moses before him, had become too powerful a leader. When Joshua commands the people, they respond: "We will do everything

68. B. Tern 16a and En Yaakov, ad loc.
69. Daniel J. Elazar, "The Book of Joshua as a Political Classic."

you have commanded us, and we will go wherever you send us."[70] We are further told that "the LORD was with Joshua, and his fame spread throughout the land."[71] Fearful of his immense and growing power and more fearful about what this portends for the future, Joshua concludes that the nation would be better suited without a king, Instead, he dies leaving a federation of twelve tribes with no single national leader that interact and cooperate with one another as necessary.

We also think that Joshua, again like Moses, was concerned with the lingering influences that Egypt had among the people. The Egyptian model of leadership was, of course, a hereditary monarchy. By not naming a successor, Joshua envisioned a system in which the people lead as opposed to being led. He hoped that this change would put the final nail in the coffin of Egyptian influences over the new tribal federation.

In a sense, the book of Joshua is one long argument against monarchy. In political science terminology, "it is an essentially republican solution designed to guarantee the continuation of limited, popular government along with renewed national energy, based upon the continued distribution of powers between the tribe, on one hand, and the national authorities, on the other."[72]

Allow us a brief digression to ask, but not answer the question, did it work? Did Joshua make the right decision?

Readers familiar with the book of Judges know that in the 400 years between the death of Joshua and the rule of David over a united nation were turbulent. There were wars with external enemies. A civil war (of sorts) that decimated the tribe of Benjamin. Communal anarchy is not an inappropriate descriptor for this epoch in Jewish history. And yet, was the monarchy that followed any better? The first Jewish king, Saul, was a man of great potential who failed because of his jealousies and paranoias. David, his successor, is considered the greatest Jewish king, but he was an adulterer and murderer. His son Solomon, despite

70. Joshua 1:16.

71. Joshua 6:27.

72. Elazar, "The Book of Joshua as a Political Classic."

his legendary wisdom, ignored the Torah's prohibitions against amassing too much wealth and marrying too many women. Worse still, he allowed his many non-Jewish wives to continue their idolatrous practices and may have even joined them. Solomon's son Rehoboam was such a despotic ruler that the kingdom splintered under his reign. Things only worsened from there.

If the period of the Judges was plagued by anarchy, the monarchies during both the First and Second Temple periods were often defined by great tyranny. Can we truthfully say which is worse? We cannot, but one thing is certain, and with this we return to the starting point of this book: in our search for the influence of Exodus on America's founding. The country's founders were justifiably concerned both about anarchy and tyranny.

First and foremost was tyranny, as explicitly spelled out in the Declaration of Independence: "The history of the present King of Great Britain is a history of repeated injuries and usurpations, all having in direct object the establishment of an absolute Tyranny over these States." Yet these leaders were not only worried about past tyrannies. They were concerned with future ones, too. James Madison perhaps said it best in *The Federalist no. 47 (1788)*: "The accumulation of all powers, legislative, executive, and judiciary, in the same hands, whether of one, a few, or many, and whether hereditary, self-appointed, or elective, may justly be pronounced the very definition of tyranny."

America's founders, like Joshua, were fearful of an all-powerful monarchy, and they thus sought to establish a republic. George Washington, perhaps more than most, understood the threat that absolute power concentrated in the hands of a single individual posed. Some claim that Washington, in the waning months of the Revolutionary War, was "offered the crown." Some think that a strongly worded rejection letter from Washington proves this theory.[73] The story, according to historians, is most likely a myth,

---

73. "Was George Washington Really Offered a Chance to Be King of the U.S.?" https://history.howstuffworks.com/historical-events/was-george-washington-really-offered-king-us.htm.

one that ranks with those of Washington cutting down a cherry tree, but Washington emerges in it as a hero once again.

Thanks to the foresight and diligence of its founders, America may have avoided the dangers of a tyrannical king in its early days, but not anarchy. From 1781 to 1789, America was a federation, similar in many ways to the federation that Joshua created with his refusal to name a successor. Its system of government was set forth in the Articles of Confederation. Under these articles, the states remained sovereign and independent (much like the twelve tribes), with Congress serving as the last resort during disputes. Congress was given the authority to make treaties and alliances, maintain armed forces, and coin money. However, the central government lacked the ability to levy taxes and regulate commerce. As such, little got done on a national level, and the emerging nation struggled to deal with the anarchy of thirteen different currencies, thirteen different trade practices and sets of tariffs, and thirteen different sets of local laws.

The situation was so precarious that Madison, Jefferson, and John Jay travelled to Mount Vernon to tell the then retired Washington that the country and the legacy he had fought so hard to build were in danger of collapse. They shared with him their vision for a new republic, one based on a new constitution, but one that could only emerge with Washington as president.[74]

America then avoided the tyranny of the monarchy by creating an executive whose powers are checked by the legislature, courts and, in some cases, the states. It avoided anarchy by abandoning a federation of thirteen states and creating a democratic federal republic. Whether knowingly or unknowingly, American's founders mimicked the leadership model of Moses and Joshua, in a sense turning twelve tribes into thirteen states, while avoiding the pitfalls of both. It is in this that we find America in Exodus.

There is a second important lesson about leadership we see in the Exodus narrative that was also incorporated by America's founders in building the new nation. It has to do with the relationship between the law and the lawgiver and is brought into sharp

74. See Joseph J. Ellis, The Quartet.

focus when Moses fervently prays to God to let him enter the Holy Land with the Jewish people.

> I pleaded with the LORD at that time, saying, "O Lord GOD, You who let Your servant see the first works of Your greatness and Your mighty hand, You whose powerful deeds no god in heaven or on earth can equal! Let me, I pray, cross over and see the good land on the other side of the Jordan, that good hill country, and the Lebanon."[75]

This is perhaps the most moving scene in the five books that bear Moses's name. After forty long years in the wilderness, he has finally brought the Jewish people to the border of Canaan.[76] Yet, the God he served so faithfully has decreed that Moses is not allowed to enter Canaan.[77] Seeing the land from across the Jordan River, Moses can no longer restrain himself. He begs. He pleads. He prays.[78] All to no avail. It is not that God is unmerciful or cruel.

75. Deuteronomy 3:23–25.

76. In chapter twelve of Genesis, when God appears to Abraham for the first time, He commands him to journey "to the land that I will show you." The rabbinic tradition understands this land to be Canaan. God then promises Abraham that He will give this land to Abraham's descendants. God ultimately repeats this explicit promise both to Abraham's son Isaac and to his grandson Jacob. Moreover, God reaffirms this promise to Moses in chapter six of Exodus when he tasks Moses with appearing before Pharoah to demand the release of the enslaved Hebrews, "I will bring you into the land which I swore to give to Abraham, Isaac, and Jacob, and I will give it to you for a possession, I the LORD."

77. The precise reason why Moses is barred from entering the land of Canaan is discussed regularly in the rabbinic literature, with many diverse explanations. The most commonly accepted theory is that because Moses hit the rock in the wilderness of Zin to bring forth water instead of speaking to it as God had commanded (Numbers 20), he was punished and not allowed to enter the Holy Land. As the rabbis framed it, "Had you spoken to the rock and it had brought forth water, I would have been sanctified before the whole congregation, for they would have said: 'What is the case with this rock which cannot speak and cannot hear and needs no maintenance? It fulfills the bidding of the Omnipresent God! How much more should we do so?'"

78. All Hebrew letters have numerical equivalents, and the letters of the word used in the biblical narrative to describe Moses's entreaties, וָאֶתְחַנַּן, total 515. The Jewish homiletic tradition learns from this appraisal that Moses offered 515 prayers to plead his case.

Rather, He is intent here on again demonstrating the true purpose of the Exodus from Egypt: not merely freedom (as we shall demonstrate in the next chapter), but the establishment of a society built upon a system of laws designed to safeguard the very freedom given to the Jewish people. As such, no one, not even the great lawgiver himself, is above the law. Thus, once the decree has been issued that Moses may not enter the Holy Land, he must be governed by that decree.

The idea that no one—not judges, not members of Congress, not the president—is above the law lies at the core of what America's founders crafted. Since the 1960s, scholars of law and politics have grown increasingly wary of the expanding powers of the president. Arthur M. Schlesinger, Jr., in 1973, even coined a phrase for this: "the Imperial Presidency." Schlesinger's thesis was simple: "As the United States became a great world power and then a superpower, the presidency acquired more war powers despite the Constitution. That reduced Congress' powers and the separation of powers, which is necessary to avoid the arbitrary use of power."[79] Nonetheless, despite the concerns that presidents have acquired powers beyond the limits of the constitution, no one believes that the president is above the law.

No one above the law? How Exodus-like!

79. Schlesinger, *The Imperial Presidency*, vii.

CHAPTER THREE

The Critical Lesson the Founders
Adopted and Followed

L ET'S BE CLEAR. THE men and women who founded America
collectively were intelligent visionaries.[1] They were well-
educated and well-read. Some were philosophers; others were
what we might today call political scientists. Among them were
business and military leaders. Many were lawyers. They were for
the most part people of means and influence. It is thus safe to say
that the idea to create a free society based on the rule of law was
not solely a product of their deep affinity for the Exodus story.
It may not have been based on Exodus at all. Yet, consciously or

1. People often and mistakenly refer to America's "Founding Fathers."
Cokie Roberts, a long-time political commentator and contributor to Na-
tional Public Radio's "Morning Edition," put this myth to rest with her book
Founding Mothers. Among the women Roberts profiles are first ladies Martha
Washington, Abigail Adams, and Dolley Madison; Benjamin Franklin's wife,
Deborah, who ran the postal service for years while Franklin was overseas; and
Esther DeBerdt Reed, an Englishwoman who, after moving with her American
husband to Boston, became so loyal to the Revolution that she wrote a rousing
newspaper article, "Sentiments of an American Woman," encouraging support
of the troops. Roberts also writes shorter entries on women who gained fame
as "warriors" for the Revolutionary cause, like Deborah Sampson (disguised
as "Robert Shurtleff," she fought in the Army until a doctor discovered her
secret) and Margaret Corbin (after her husband was killed in the Battle of Fort
Washington, she held his artillery position despite suffering gunshot wounds).

unconsciously, these individuals built a nation following the most fundamental lesson of Exodus.

Without a doubt, the Exodus saga is about freedom, and the Jew's liberation from Egypt has given hope to multitudes of enslaved peoples. One need look no farther than the African-American spiritual "Go Down, Moses" to see how true this is. As the song famously states:

> When Israel was in Egypt's land,
> let my people go;
> oppressed so hard they could not stand,
> let my people go.
> **Refrain:**
> Go down, Moses,
> way down in Egypt's land;
> tell old Pharaoh to let my people go![2]

The Jewish rabbinic tradition does not ignore the obvious. Exodus is a story about the longing for freedom and its ultimate obtainment: a notion that the rabbis reenforced by crafting seemingly countless rituals to mark Passover as "the festival of freedom." As a result, Jews around the world commemorate this freedom every spring at their Passover seders.[3] Nonetheless, this very same tradition understands that freedom was not the goal of the Exodus from Egypt. The Talmudic sages explain:

> And it says, "And the tablets were the work of God, and the writing was the writing of God, graven upon the tablets" (Exodus 32:16). Read not *haruth* [graven] but

---

2. This spiritual was probably well known before its first publication in sheet music form in December 1861 as "The Song of the Contrabands" subtitled "O! Let my people Go." One Virginia chaplain, Rev. L. C. Lockwood, who assisted escaped slaves prior to the Civil War, observed that this song was sung by fugitive slaves as early as 1853. C. Michael Hawn, "History of Hymns: 'Go Down, Moses.'"

3. According to Rabbi Emanuel Feldman, Passover is the most widely observed ritual even among Jews who are otherwise ritually non-observant. See "The Odd and Instructive Habits of Non-Observant Jews: A Look at Berit Milah and Pesah."

heruth [freedom]. For there is no free man but one that occupies himself with the study of the Torah.[4]

What are the rabbis trying to communicate with this statement? It is not merely a clever word pun (read not *haruth* [graven] but *heruth* [freedom]). It is instead a deeply insightful observation about the true nature of the Exodus from Egypt and the freedom that it bought.

How so?

If you look closely at the biblical story of Exodus, you will see that the Hebrew word used for freedom throughout the narrative is *chofesh*.[5] The word is related to *chafetz*, "desire," and *chapess*, "seek." *Chofesh/chofshi* is thus the appropriate term to describe the status of a freed slave. Here freedom means that the individual can do whatever he or she likes. There is no longer an owner or a master to order him or her around. As Rabbi Jonathan Sacks explains it, "*Chofesh* is the freedom to pursue your desires. It is what philosophers call negative liberty. It means the absence of coercion."[6]

The absence of coercion would seem to describe the condition of the Jewish people upon their departure from Egypt. Yet, the rabbis reject this term when discussing post-Exodus Jews. The rabbis understood that the Exodus from Egypt was intended to achieve more than freedom from the brutalities of slavery. They saw that God's plan for the Jewish people entailed more than freedom itself. This led them to intuit the need for a new term for freedom—*heruth*—because they realized that while *chofesh* is a fine descriptor for individual freedom, it does not connote collective freedom. Why is this? Because a society in which everyone is free to do what they like, no matter what the consequences, cannot truly be a free society.[7] Stated differently, the complete freedom

4. Pirkei Avot 6:2.

5. The Torah uses a different word for freedom, *dror*, in connection with the Jubilee year (Leviticus 25:10). Rabbi Jonathan Sacks discusses the difference between the two terms in a 2012 article entitled "The Birth of a New Freedom."

6. Sacks, "The Birth of a New Freedom."

7. Sacks, "The Birth of a New Freedom."

enjoyed by an individual when it comes with anarchy is not the model for society that emerges from the Exodus narrative. Law—the rules and regulations that create an ordered society—undergirds the model of freedom to which both Jewish and American societies subscribe.

There is more to this than an exercise in linguistics. Again, look closely at the biblical narrative. After ten devasting plagues, Pharaoh orders the Jews to leave immediately, and they indeed depart in great haste. In fact, they left so hastily that there wasn't enough time for their dough to rise.[8] Despite this sense of urgency, the Jewish people do not head directly to the land that had been promised to them by God. Instead, they march for seven weeks through the Sinai Wilderness until they reach Mount Sinai. Their purpose? To receive God's laws. To what end? At Sinai, God explains in unequivocal terms the true purpose of the exodus:

> Now then, if you will obey Me faithfully and keep My covenant, you shall be My treasured possession among all the peoples. Indeed, all the earth is Mine, but you shall be to Me a kingdom of priests and a holy nation.[9]

Nowhere is freedom found in this exhortation from God. God is instead making it clear that the Jewish people were not liberated simply to become free. They were liberated to become "a holy nation," that is, a nation committed to building a society based on God's laws and mandates. Freedom is just a necessary precondition to creating a law-abiding society. This is the insight and logic that underlies the rabbinic statement, read not *haruth* [graven] but *heruth* [freedom].[10]

---

8. This, of course, is one of the reasons Jews eat matza at their seders, to recall the haste with which they left Egypt.

9. Exodus 19:5–6.

10. Rabbi Joseph B. Soloveitchik, one of the greatest Jewish thinkers and philosophers of the twentieth century, clearly saw that redemption from Egypt involved more than a transition from slavery to freedom. As he put it, "liberation meant throwing off man's yoke and willing embracing God's yoke." Besdin, "On Freedom and Slavery," 205.

This, too, is the critical lesson that America's founders took from the Exodus story.

Like the Exodus saga before it, the American Revolution was a unique phenomenon in the modern era. This is not to say that there were no rebellions and revolutions after it. There were. So many in fact that modern social science scholarship has advanced numerous distinct theories that explain why revolutions occur.[11] What sets apart the American Revolution was the synergistic linking between freedom and the law, something seemingly absent in subsequent revolutions, but something that goes to the heart of the Exodus story.

Freedom is something often associated with America, as is Jefferson's iconic language in the Declaration of Independence about "life, liberty, and the pursuit of happiness." What is striking in this language is its emphasis on the individual and his or her personal freedoms. Yet, this is not enough, because individualism is not a legal system.

For Jefferson and America's other founders, protecting freedom was a given, and after the failure of the Articles of Confederation, America's political leaders understood that a new governmental and legal paradigm was needed. To be sure, they had seen how freedom, when divorced from the law, could not endure.

The Constitution was and continues to be the foundation that safeguards freedom in the United States. The Constitution itself does not address what might be considered personal freedoms or rights, save for three exceptions set forth in Article One, Section Nine.[12] The personal freedoms Americans often take for granted

11. See, for example, Jack A. Goldstone, *Revolutions* and Gizachew Tiruneh "Social Revolutions."

12. In broad terms, these three exceptions protect American citizens from being jailed without charges being filed, from being declared guilty of a crime without a trial, and from retroactively being charged with a crime for an act that was not criminal when performed. One obvious issue involving personal freedoms ignored entirely by the Constitution was slavery. In fact, the only decisions made by the drafters of the Constitution regarding slavery were both cynical and immoral. First was the infamous "Three-fifths Compromise," an agreement between delegates from the Northern and the Southern states that three-fifths of the enslaved population would be counted for determining

are, for the most part, prescribed by the Bill of Rights. American courts have played a major role in shaping these rights, especially with regards to the scope and application of those rights found in the Bill of Rights.

The Court's efforts to define and protect our fundamental rights is a major reason why many Americans see the Supreme Court as the guardian of individual rights.[13] The extent to which this perception is justified can be a topic of heated debate, but one fact is indisputable: the Court is not the sole protector of individual freedoms and liberties. The other two branches of the American government—the Legislative and the Executive—are involved, too, as is the public. "Even after the Supreme Court issues a constitutional decision, the elected branches and the general public are at liberty to consider policies contrary to what the Court has decided. Although it may take decades, nonjudicial forces can prevail."[14] This perspective was concisely articulated by the late Ruth Bader Ginsburg when she appeared before the Senate Judiciary Committee on July 20, 1993, as a nominee to the Supreme Court: "Justices do not guard constitutional rights alone. Courts share that profound responsibility with Congress, the president, the states, and the people." [15]

At this point, it is appropriate to step back and reflect on the American notion of freedom and its interaction with the law. Let us start by conceding that we will most likely find little agreement

---

direct taxation and representation in the House of Representatives. As to the question of slavery itself, the Constitution is strikingly silent. It merely allowed for a ban on the importation of slaves but forbade the ban from taking effect prior to January 1, 1808. In practical terms, this ban did nothing to alleviate the lot of those enslaved in America. It merely made "breeding" slaves a highly lucrative business, which in turn meant that thousands of black families in the South were torn apart as spouses and children were sold indiscriminately to other slave holders.

13. It remains to be seen how the Supreme Court's recent overturning of Roe v. Wade will affect this perception remains.

14. Fisher, 66.

15. Fisher, 66.

to the precise meaning of the terms "freedom" and "liberty." An anecdote from well-known historian Eric Foner proves that point.

Foner writes about the Freedom Train, which in 1947 and 1948 travelled to more than 300 American cities to commemorate the 160th anniversary of the signing of the U.S. Constitution. It was a traveling exhibition that contained 133 historical documents, including the Mayflower Compact, the Declaration of Independence, and the Gettysburg Address. Foner notes that "after leaving the train, visitors were exhorted to dedicate themselves to American values by taking the Freedom Pledge and adding their names to a Freedom Scroll." He goes on to describe the reaction to the train:

> The powerful grassroots response to the train, wrote *The New Republic*, revealed a deep popular hunger for "tangible evidence of American freedom." Behind the scenes, however, the Freedom Train demonstrated that the precise meaning of freedom was hardly uncontroversial. The liberal staff members at the National Archives who proposed the initial list of documents had included the Wagner Act of 1935, which guaranteed labor's right to collective bargaining, and President Roosevelt's Four Freedoms speech of 1941 listing freedom of speech and religion, freedom from fear, and the vaguely socialistic freedom from want as the Allies' aims in World War II. These, however, were eliminated by the more conservative American Heritage Foundation. Also omitted were the Fourteenth and Fifteenth Amendments to the constitution, which had granted civil and political rights to blacks after the Civil War, and Roosevelt's order of 1941 establishing the Fair Employment Practices Commission. In the end, nothing on the train referred to organized labor or any 20th-century social legislation and of the 133 documents, only three related to blacks: the Emancipation Proclamation, Thirteenth Amendment, and a 1776 letter criticizing slavery. [16]

16. Eric Foner, *The Story of American Freedom*, 250.

If this is the case, what agreement can there be when it comes to defining an American perspective on freedom and liberty? What can we say with confidence about either concept?

In our opinion, there are actually a few things.

First, Americans are consistently aspirational in their national declarations, be it Jefferson's "we hold these truths to be self-evident," the stated goal found in the Preamble to the U.S. Constitution "to form a more perfect Union," or Lincoln's ringing cry at Gettysburg "that government of the people, by the people, for the people, shall not perish from the earth." However, the reality is that Americans do not always live up to their lofty aspirations (but who does?). Even so, throughout the country's history, there has always been a subset of the population, sometimes larger than at other times, that has pushed and prodded the country to do more and be better. There is an argument to be made that this group has grown larger and more determined in recent years. Look at the increased emphasis on women's rights, civil rights and social justice, gay and trans rights, even economic rights, all of which seem to dominate social and political conversations to varying degrees.

Second, no matter where the focus might be, Americans tend to emphasize the rights and freedoms of the individual. This was true for the Bill of Rights, just as it is true for lobbyists and activists from groups ranging from the NRA to Black Lives Matter. Just look at the language they use: "my right to bear arms;" "my right to choose to have an abortion;" "my right to marry the person of my choice;" "my right to post or tweet whatever message or speech I want;" or even "my right not to wear a mask and not get vaccinated."[17]

In his inaugural address, John Kennedy declared: "Ask not what your country can do for you. Ask what you can do for your

---

17. The contrast between this perspective and the Jewish approach to individual rights was made very clear by Lord Rabbi Immanuel Jakobovits: "In Judaism we know of no intrinsic rights. Indeed, there is no word for rights in the very language of the Hebrew Bible and of the classic sources of Jewish law. In the moral vocabulary of the Jewish discipline of life we speak of human duties, not of human rights, of obligations not entitlement." Jakobovits, *The Timely and the Timeless*, 128.

country." A truly aspirational thought. However, when it comes to individual freedoms and liberties, most Americans are likely to ignore Kennedy and instead ask, or perhaps even demand to know, what their country can do for them.[18]

This emphasis on the individual, as we will discuss in the next chapter, stands in sharp contrast to the Jewish view of freedom. Freedom in Jewish thought is neither freedom of the individual nor freedom from responsibility. For a Jew, freedom encompasses commitment and devotion to God, to the study of His laws, and to the Jewish people (be it the nation as a whole or one's smaller, local community). These in turn are presumed to exist only in a setting where there is an equally strong commitment to the law because, in the Jewish worldview, it is the law that makes each of them possible.

---

18. This attitude may not be unique to America. In his book, *The WEIRDest People in the World,* Joseph Henrich amassed hundreds of pages of data to on Western, Educated, Industrialized, Rich and Democratic values. He found that, "We WEIRD people are highly individualistic, self-obsessed, control-oriented, nonconformist and analytical. We focus on ourselves—our attributes, accomplishments and aspirations—over our relationships and social roles." In reflecting on Henrich's work, David Brooks of the *New York Times* wrote that many people around the world look at American ideas on a variety of topics as "foreign or repellent." Brooks continued, "The idea that it's up to each person to choose one's own identity and values—that seems ridiculous to many. The idea that the purpose of education is to inculcate critical thinking skills so students can liberate themselves from the ideas they received from their parents and communities—that seems foolish to many." Brooks may be correct, but we believe that what he describes is happening nonetheless. "Globalization Is Over. The Global Culture Wars Have Begun," *New York Times*, April 8, 2022, https://www.nytimes.com/2022/04/08/opinion/globalization-global-culture-war.html?referringSource=articleShare.

CHAPTER FOUR

Where Judaism's Founders Differed

A MERICA'S FOUNDERS, LIKE THEIR Jewish counterparts, intuited the central lesson of Exodus, namely, that freedom is a necessary precondition to creating a law-abiding society. Without freedom, law is not possible, but freedom does not insure law. Yet, there is a profound difference between America and Judaism—specifically, in terms of the essential focus of law.

Let's start with the American legal system.

Quite simply, the Constitution "does not aim to instruct people on the virtues, or the content of happiness, or the path to salvation."[1] Not because virtue is irrelevant or because happiness has no content, but rather, the Constitution presupposes that the people, as individuals and through the various associations and groups they form, will pursue good.[2] Recognizing this,, the Constitution establishes a framework for how American citizens can maintain a society where each "has the liberty to pursue, consistent with a like liberty for others, virtue, happiness, and salvation in the way each regards as fitting."[3]

Said differently, the Constitution defines what is legal, not what is moral.

1. Berkowitz, "The Court."
2. Berkowitz, "The Court."
3. Berkowitz, "The Court."

To underscore this point, one need only consider the Treaty of Tripoli of 1797, negotiated under George Washington, approved unanimously by the US Senate, and signed by President John Adams. It states quite emphatically that "[t]he government of the United States of America is not, in any sense, founded on the Christian Religion." When taken in tandem with the First Amendment, which Jefferson revered "as building a wall of separation between church and state,"[4] we see that America's founders sought to establish "a secular republic ruled by democratic laws, not sectarian faith; a nation whose government based its authority upon 'we, the people' and not commandments handed down by distant gods."[5]

In contradistinction, Judaism has always believed that law has never been, nor can it be, uncoupled from religious morality. The Talmudic sages saw this to be true even before the giving of the Torah at Mount Sinai. As proof, they point to the statement God makes to Noah after the flood: "I now establish My covenant with you and your offspring to come."[6] These rabbinic scholars saw in this verse the basics of humankind's first legal system in which Noah and his descendants were commanded to establish laws prohibiting the cursing of God, idolatry, illicit sexuality, bloodshed, robbery, and eating flesh from a living animal.[7]

One can see in these first commandments the beginnings of an emphasis on religious morality. Take, for example, the prohibition against illicit sexuality. The Talmudic sages and later scholars understood that illicit sexual relationships included one's mother, one's father's wife, another man's wife, a man's sister from the same mother, homosexual unions, and bestiality.[8] These are not

---

4. Jefferson penned this iconic phrase in a letter to Danbury Baptist Association dated January 1, 1802. https://founders.archives.gov/documents/Jefferson/01-36-02-0152-0006.

5. Zuckerman and Seidel, "The Supreme Court's right-wing Catholics are destroying true religious freedom."

6. Genesis 9:9.

7. Sanhedrin 56a; cf. Tosefta Avodah Zarah 8:4 and Genesis Rabbah 34:8.

8. Maimonides, Laws of Kings, 9:5.

matters typically proscribed in most legal codes, certainly not in America in 2022.

Some rabbinic scholars see these seven Noahide laws as touching areas that today are frequently described as matters of social justice. One medieval Bible commentator, Nahmanides, sums up this view as follows: "In my opinion, the laws which the Noahides were to establish according to their seven commandments is not only to establish courts in each town, but that they were also commanded concerning theft, abuse, usury, labor relations, damages, loans, business, and the like."[9]

There are even philosophers who see in the Noahide laws a sort of universal, natural morality. Hermann Cohen,[10] as one example, argued that these laws demonstrated that "ancient Judaism recognized that citizenship in the state should not have any religious prerequisites, that the only prerequisites should be moral, namely, a commitment to obey civil law—Even the prohibition of idolatry is interpreted as a repudiation of the immoral practices so intimately associated with idolatry in ancient times."[11]

The revelation at Sinai makes the link between law and religious morality both stronger and more paradoxical.

True, there seems nothing innately immoral about eating a ham sandwich or cross breeding a sheep and a goat, but both are forbidden by Torah law.[12] What is of critical importance is that all Jewish law falls under the rubric of "meta-commandments." Perhaps the best known of these is set forth in Deuteronomy, where the Jewish people are commanded to "Do what is right and good in the sight of the LORD."[13]

9. Nahmanides, Commentary to Genesis 34:13.

10. Cohen, a German Jewish philosopher, was one of the founders of the Marburg school of neo-Kantianism, and he is often held to be among most important Jewish philosophers of the nineteenth century.

11. David Novak, "Universal Moral Law in the Theology of Hermann Cohen."

12. The prohibition against eating pork is found in Leviticus 11:27, while the prohibition against cross breeding animals is found in Mishnah Kil'ayim 1:6.

13. Deuteronomy 6:18.

Let us ask here, what does this mean in practical terms, especially since Deuteronomy does not define either what is "right" or what is "good" in the eyes of the Lord?

To answer this question and, more importantly, to understand the fundamental link between law and morality in Judaism, we must turn to the Talmudic sages for their insights. Let us begin with the following incidents as described in Bava Metzia 83a:

> A man was once moving a barrel of wine in the manor of Mahuza, and broke it on a projection of Mahuza: so he came before Raba. Said he to him: The manor of Mahuza is a frequented place: go and bring evidence, then you are free from liability. Thereupon R. Yosef, his son, said to him: In accordance with whom [is your verdict]? With Issi?—Yes, said he, in accordance with Issi; and we agree with him.
>
> A man instructed his neighbor. "Go and buy me four hundred barrels of wine." So he went and bought [them] for him; subsequently, however, he came before him and said, "I bought you the four hundred barrels of wine, but they turned sour." So he came before Raba. "When four hundred barrels of wine turn sour," said he to him, "the facts should be widely known. Go and bring proof that originally, when bought, the wine was sound, then will you be free from liability." R. Yosef, his son, observed to him: In accordance with whom [is your verdict]? With Issi?—Yes, said he, in accordance with Issi; and we agree with him.

In both cases, an individual appears before Raba seeking a ruling on his liability vis-à-vis damages that resulted from his actions. And in both cases, Raba declines to rule on the matter. Instead, he offers advice to the individual how to prove that he was not negligent and thus not liable. Not the behavior one would expect from a rabbi positioned to render a legal decision, but one entirely consistent with the notion of doing what is "good and right."[14]

14. By way of contrast, consider the ruling of the Supreme Court in *Shinn v. Ramirez* (issued on May 23, 2022). The defendant in this case was sentenced to death for the sexual assault and killing of a four-year-old girl. However, his court-appointed trial court lawyer did not investigate the facts of the case.

The next case cited by the Talmud is even more telling.

> Some porters [negligently] broke a barrel of wine belonging to Rabbah son of R. Huna. Thereupon he seized their garments; so they went and complained to Rav. "Return them their garments," he ordered. "Is that the law?" he enquired. "Even so," he replied: "**That you may walk in the way of good men.**" (Tehillim 2:20) Their garments having been returned, they observed. "We are poor men, have worked all day, and are in need: are we to get nothing?" "Go and pay them," he ordered. "Is that the law?" he asked. "Even so," was his reply: "**and keep the path of the righteous.**" (Tehillim 2:20). [emphasis added]

In this case, the rabbi who was posed to issue a legal ruling seems to instead resort to ethical principles in order to improve upon the law. In his eyes, following the strict letter of the law

---

Arizona law (where the defendant was charged and convicted) does not allow the first post-conviction appeal to raise the question of ineffective assistance of counsel. On the second appeal, the appellate lawyer did not raise the question either. Only when federal public defenders were brought into the case for a federal court hearing did they examine the medical evidence and consult experts, who later testified that the injuries inflicted on the child occurred not when the prosecution claimed, but at a time when Jones was nowhere near the child and could not have inflicted them. In other words, evidence that would have conclusively proven the innocence of the defendant was never considered during his trial and subsequent appeal due to ineffective and inept legal counsel. A federal appeals court unanimously agreed that the defendant was entitled to a new trial and that this previously undisclosed evidence should be considered. Arizona appealed this ruling, and the Supreme Court held in its favor, despite a 2012 ruling by the court stating that when a state court "substantially" interferes with a defendant's constitutional right to be represented by counsel, the defendant, with a new lawyer, may appeal to federal court to show that he was denied his right to effective counsel. Writing for the majority in the 2022 case, Justice Clarence Thomas said that federal courts may not hear "new evidence" obtained after conviction to show how deficient the trial or appellate lawyer in state court was. To allow such evidence to be presented in federal court, he said, "encourages prisoners to sandbag state courts," depriving the states of "the finality that is essential to both the retributive and deterrent function of criminal law." In our view, it would be difficult to find a starker contrast between American and Jewish jurisprudence or between doing "what is legal" versus doing "what is right."

would not have been sufficient because it would not have been the good or the right thing to do.

Rabbah's approach in this matter is subsequently embraced by the Talmudic sages. Moreover, it can be argued that the Talmud never saw following the strict letter of the law to be sufficient. To prove the point, its sages went so far as to claim that Jerusalem was destroyed because judgments were based strictly on the law and did not go beyond the strict line of justice.[15]

On what basis would the Talmudic sages determine that they could and should go beyond the letter of the law? This is where the exhortation, the meta-command, to "do what is good and right in the eyes of the LORD," comes into play.

The Talmud uses this verse in several well-known instances. For example, the sages required individuals to return objects that they find even if the object was lost in a place where the owner clearly would have given up any hope of its recovery (e.g., if it fell into the sea).[16] In such a case, there is no legal obligation at all. Nonetheless, the sages demanded the return of the lost object!

What we see from these teachings is that, in Jewish law, the legal content of the law is fundamentally connected to ethics and morality. In other words, whether a defendant can or cannot be prosecuted for an action may be less important than knowing about whether it is the "right" thing to do.[17]

The coupling of law and morality is the most significant difference between Jewish and American jurisprudence. Yet, for all its significance, it does not run counter to our thesis, namely, that preserving the law is a prerequisite to preserving freedom in both societies. Here's why. From the perspective of individual members

15. The Talmud in Bava Metzia 30b posits the following: "Rebbe Yochanan stated, Jerusalem was only destroyed because they judged according to the law of the Torah. [The students objected] Should then they have judged according to the laws of the sorcerers?! Rather, they insisted narrowly on the strict Torah law, and did not go beyond the letter of the law."

16. Bava Metzia 24b.

17. This also explains why, in his commentary to Leviticus 19:2, Nachmanides famously notes that one can follow the letter of the law and still be considered a "vile person within the permissible realm of the Torah."

of either society, does it matter if murder is illegal because it runs counter to some notion of a Lockean social contract or because it was deemed immoral by the one true God above? We don't think it does. Laws that ban harmful activities such as murder or assault or robbery keep people safe and, by extension, keep them free.

Secularists may well argue that rationality makes for better laws. Theologists may contend that a moral underpinning to the law yields a superior system. We believe that either can suffice to safeguard the rights and freedoms of the individual.

A concluding thought is in order.

The Jewish legal system, as we have seen, is based on a very different question. It does not simply ask, "is it legal?" Rather, in addition whether it is legal, it asks "is it right?" This question itself is reflected in the Hebrew term for Jewish law, *halakha*.

The English word "law" is defined as a system of rules that a particular country or community recognizes as regulating the actions of its members and which it may enforce by the imposition of penalties. Was *halakha* recognized and enforced by Jewish courts in ancient times (and even today in certain legal matters)? Certainly. Was it enforced by monetary and even capital penalties? Yes. Nonetheless, the term *halakha* connotes far more than its English language counterpart. The root of the term *halakha* means "go" or "walk." *Halakha*, then, is the "way" a Jew is directed to behave in every aspect of life, encompassing civil, criminal, and religious law. It is, at its core, a fusion of law and ethics. It demands that a Jew do what is right as well as what is lawful.

What does this mean in practical terms?

The Torah repeatedly commands us to care for the widow, the orphan, the stranger, and the oppressed. The rabbinic tradition teaches us again and again of the importance of "going beyond the letter of the law" in order to do that which is "just and right in the eyes of the Lord." This question (and the communal recognition that it must be answered in the affirmative) has meant that, over the centuries, Jewish communities have crafted intricate social safety nets, ranging from Eastern European "community chests" in the old world to contemporary North American Federations and free-loan societies.

The enduring nature of both the American and Jewish legal systems underscore their commonalities. However, their divergent approaches to what is the core of their legal systems (is it legal or is it right) shows that, despite the extent to which the Exodus narrative influenced and continues to influence the American legal system, America has yet to reach the status of "the promised land." To arrive at that "more perfect union" envisioned in the Preamble to the US Constitution, Americans need to ask their legislators and their jurists more often, "is it right?" Is this the type of outcome that will "promote the general Welfare and secure the Blessings of Liberty to ourselves and our Posterity"?

Only then will America truly and fully be found in Exodus.

CHAPTER FIVE

Why the Exodus Narrative Still Matters

F REEDOM IS SOMETHING MOST Americans take for granted and with good reason. Thanks to the guarantees regarding personal freedoms set forth in the Bill of Rights, Americans are justified in their belief that they live in one of the freest countries in the world. They are free to say and wear whatever they like. They are free to marry whomever they want. They are free to worship any god they choose in the setting of their choice. Americans have a free press.[1] They enjoy an unsurpassed freedom of speech, including the right to freely and safely criticize their political leaders.[2]

---

1. As Jefferson wrote to his colleague Edward Carrington from Paris in 1789, "were it left to me to decide whether we should have a government without newspapers or newspapers without a government, I should not hesitate a moment to prefer the latter." https://oll.libertyfund.org/quote/jefferson-s-preference-for-newspapers-without-government-over-government-without-newspapers-1787.

2. As we were making our final edits, the US Supreme Court issued its ruling in *Dobbs v. Jackson Women's Health Organization*. In its ruling, the Court held that the Fourteenth Amendment conferred no privacy rights that would grant women a constitutional right to abortion. It therefore overruled both *Roe v. Wade* (1973) and *Planned Parenthood v. Casey* (1992). The decision leaves abortion rights or restrictions to be defined at the state level. Given our comparisons between the American and Jewish legal systems, it seems worthwhile to briefly ponder what Jewish law might have to say vis-à-vis the abortion law of the United States or of any particular state. We believe that four basic ideas could answer this question. First, Jews have no halakhic obligation

These freedoms have shaped America's foreign policy for decades. Much of the Cold War was driven by America's desire to contain communism and to protect democracy and freedom around the world. America's post-9/11 efforts at regime change and nation building similarly reflected a desire to introduce freedom to the oppressed peoples of Afghanistan and Iraq. America's enthusiasm for the Arab Spring in 2011 was an extension of these desires, and many Americans cheered the pro-democracy uprisings in Tunisia, Morocco, Syria, Libya, Egypt, and Bahrain. In 2022, Americans stand united in their desire to help Ukraine in its war against Russian aggression in order to preserve its freedom.

In hindsight, these policies miss the mark. The Iron Curtain did fall in 1989, marking an end to the Cold War, but how many countries in Eastern Europe, including Russia itself, are truly free today? America's attempts at regime change in Iraq and Afghanistan were utter failures. Iraq's post-2003 political system has been characterized by instability driven by many factors, including ethnic and sectarian tensions, interventions by neighboring countries, and security challenges created by terrorist groups, militias, and gangs. The situation in Afghanistan is worse still. The Taliban regained control of the country in 2021 after the withdrawal of the last American troops. The Taliban quickly moved to instill Islamic law and roll back the freedoms many Afghans (especially Afghani

---

to encourage non-Jews to observe Noahide law. Second, even in the absence of a technical obligation, doing so may sometimes be a wise idea and good policy. Third, since encouraging certain conduct can also sometimes be unwise politically and practically for the Jewish community, it sometimes trumps the priority to encourage Noahide law observance when its cost is high. Finally, since abortion is prohibited for Gentiles under Noahide Law more strictly than for Jews under Jewish Law—a rare case where Jewish Law is more permissive than Noahide Law—it is almost impossible to fashion a secular law regulating abortion which is consistent with both Jewish Law and Noahide law. Thus, we think that the proper Jewish framework for thinking about secular abortion law is not Judaism's approach to abortion but rather its embrace of individuals' freedom to act in many life and death matters in accordance with their assessment of their personal circumstances. See Michael J. Broyde, "What Does Jewish Law Think American Abortion Law Ought To Be?"

women) had enjoyed subsequent to the arrival of American troops in their country in 2001.

This all begs the question, is freedom inevitable? Is it always desirable? Americans tend to think so, but that does not necessarily make it true. We therefore want to ponder this question as we conclude our examination of the interaction between freedom and the law.

In 1995, on the fiftieth anniversary of the United Nations, Pope John Paul II gave an address to the UN General Assembly in which he argued that there is indeed a "universal longing for freedom." He said:

> On the threshold of a new millennium, we are witnessing an extraordinary global acceleration of that quest for freedom which is one of the great dynamics of human history. This phenomenon is not limited to any one part of the world; nor is it the expression of any single culture. Men and women throughout the world, even when threatened by violence, have taken the risk of freedom, asking to be given a place in social, political, and economic life which is commensurate with their dignity as free human beings. This universal longing for freedom is truly one of the distinguishing marks of our time.[3]

We think that most Americans would agree with the Pope's sentiments. From Patrick Henry ("I know not what course others may take, but as for me, give me liberty, or give me death!") to Malcolm X ("A man who believes in freedom will do anything under the sun to acquire, or preserve his freedom."), Americans are often quick to subscribe to the idea that freedom is precious and always worth pursuing.

Some hold that this ideal far predates its American iteration. They maintain that this yearning for freedom was already common in classical Greece, where "'revolutions' were considered a normal way of assuming power by differing regimes. They occurred

3. Address of His Holiness John Paul II, United Nations Headquarters, October 5, 1995, http://www.vatican.va/content/john-paul-ii/en/speeches/1995/october/documents/hf_jp-ii_spe_05101995_address-to-uno.html.

whenever democratic, oligarchic, and monarchic regimes alternated in assuming power, and such alternation of political power often came through violence."[4]

Yet others would argue that the longing for freedom comes with a very large caveat. Individuals long for freedom when they are free from need, meaning that their basic needs (food, clothing, and shelter) are readily available to most of the population. Nelson Mandela, one of the great freedom-fighters of the twentieth century, understood this when he said, "While poverty persists, there is no true freedom."[5]

History has repeatedly shown that starving, naked people rarely raise the cry for freedom. Nevertheless, Americans tend to assume that even starving people desire freedom, but can we reasonably say that freedom is always the best outcome?

No, we cannot.

Consider the case of Mussolini's Italy. Under Mussolini, the Italian Fascists imposed totalitarian rule and crushed political and intellectual opposition, all while promoting economic modernization, traditional social values, and a rapprochement with the Roman Catholic Church. Best of all, it is often said, Mussolini made the trains run on time.[6] This was seemingly a worthy trade off to

4. Gizachew Tiruneh, "Social Revolutions: Their Causes, Patterns, and Phases," 1.

5. These words were part of a speech Mandela delivered in London's Trafalgar Square in 2005. https://www.globalcitizen.org/en/content/nelson-mandela-quotes-poverty-injustice-peace/.

6. The website Snopes.com, known for fact-checking and debunking myths of all kinds, states that Mussolini did no such thing. This is how the website describes Mussolini's accomplishments in this area: "Mussolini needed to convince the people of Italy that fascism was indeed a system that worked to their benefit. Thus was born the myth of fascist efficiency, with the train as its symbol. The word was spread that Mussolini had turned the dilapidated Italian railway system into one that was the envy of all Europe, featuring trains that were both dependable and punctual. In Mussolini's Italy, all the trains ran on time. Well, not quite. The Italian railway system had fallen into a rather delapidated state during World War I, and it did improve a good deal during the 1920s, but Mussolini was disingenuous in taking credit for the changes: much of the repair work had been performed before Mussolini and the 1922 fascist takeover. More importantly (to the claim at hand), those who actually

many citizens of Italy, at least until Mussolini allied Italy with Nazi Germany. Of course, it never was a wise idea.

An example that hits closer to home for many Americans is is Saddam's Iraq.

Chris Maume, a radio columnist for the British publication *Independent*, tackled this issue as it pertained to Iraq, both during and after the Saddam years. Here is his perspective, and it is one that can be found in dozens of anecdotal accounts. He wrote:

> There was universal health care in Iraq, and universal education. Few people were well off but nobody, as far as I could tell, starved.
>
> True, all we had to go on was the English-language newspaper the Baghdad Observer, with its daily cover stories about Saddam's latest visit to an adoring Kurd village (this was before the notorious gas attack on Halabja), but national misery is difficult to keep off the streets, and people seemed happy.
>
> Baghdad was noisy and mucky and full of building sites, but it was bustling and thriving. There wasn't a huge amount in the shops, but people had all they needed to get by. . . .
>
> So Iraq, when I was there, was a fully functioning state in which it was possible to live a fulfilled life. I'm aware that what I'm saying may be the equivalent of observing that Hitler made the trains run on time. But I wonder how many Iraqis today—particularly those in flight, with nothing but their children and a few hastily gathered possessions—look back on the Saddam years.[7]

A more blunt assessment framed it this way: "The majority of people before—Sunni and Shiite—did not like the regime . . . But many people, when they compare between the situation under

---

lived in Italy during the Mussolini era have borne testimony that the Italian railway's legendary adherence to timetables was far more myth than reality." David Mikkelson, "Mussolini and On Time Trains."

7. Chris Maume, "It was better to live in Iraq under Saddam."

Saddam Hussein and now, find maybe their life under Saddam Hussein was better."[8]

Even the Hebrews, whom God Himself liberated from Egypt, seemed filled with nostalgia for the "easy life" that they had in Pharaoh's Egypt: "The Israelites wept and said, 'If only we had meat to eat! We remember the fish that we used to eat free in Egypt, the cucumbers, the melons, the leeks, the onions, and the garlic. Now our gullets are shriveled. There is nothing at all! Nothing but this manna to look to!'"[9]

In the end, is there a universal longing for freedom? Perhaps. Is freedom inevitable? In the right circumstances, probably. Does freedom always produce a positive outcome? Depends on who you ask. Yet, one thing is clear. For the British colonialists living in North America in the 1700s and the Hebrews enslaved in ancient Egypt, freedom was a much-desired commodity (even though there were times when both groups questioned their actions in seeking freedom).

While we remain convinced that freedom continues to be a desired outcome, we are far less certain that it is still an enduring one. It seems that the legal and political systems in both Israel and America are facing unique if not unprecedented challenges. In our view, it is possible that these challenges are poised to threaten the basic freedoms enjoyed by both countries.

Between 2019 and 2022, Israel had five national elections. These elections resulted in a political stalemate leaving them without a national budget during a worldwide pandemic. Its former prime minister, Benjamin Netanyahu, faced criminal charges of bribery, fraud, and breach of trust. Israel's religious court system, which is responsible for marriages and conversions, faced increasing criticism and calls for it to be stripped of those responsibilities. Israel's secular court system also had its critics, and it faced both domestic and international pressure to reform itself to grant

---

8. Jan Arraf, "15 Years After U.S. Invasion, Some Iraqis Are Nostalgic For Saddam Hussein Era."

9. Numbers 11:4–6.

greater equality to Israel's Arab citizens and the Palestinians under its control.

On the other hand, this situation in America evokes equal levels of concern and pessimism.

America today is a polarized country. Even more so now, according to many pundits and political analysts, than at any time since the Civil War. Not so long ago, Americans could engage their families and friends in a wide range of discussions on any number of topics. Consensus was not always reached, but civility was the order of the day. No longer. Today, if I disagree with your opinion or your worldview, I am not merely wrong or misinformed—I am stupid and evil.[10]

Agreement on facts now seems beyond many Americans. Was January 6th "an armed insurrection"[11] or was it just "a normal tourist visit," as Rep. Andrew S. Clyde (R-GA) claims?[12] Is climate change a real danger to be addressed now or a hoax perpetrated by radical leftists who wish to undermine the foundations of the U.S. economy? How one answers such questions reflects the news sources one turns to. Viewers of CNN and readers of *The New York Times* subscribe to one set of "facts." Those who rely on Fox News or One America News Network believe in an alternative "set of facts." For example, since January 6, 2021, Tucker Carlson of FOX News, who anchors the highest rated of all the cable news shows, has said that the events of January 6 were "not an insurrection."

10. See, for example, "Americans can't have political conversations," https://www.breezejmu.org/opinion/opinion-americans-can-t-have-political-conversations/article_20ba4526-2405-11e9-89b2-5b60869dfef9.html; "Civil discourse is disappearing in America," http://www.dailynebraskan.com/opinion/herbert-civil-discourse-is-disappearing-in-america/article_89da698a-09c5-11eb-bbdb-ff9faa4c3049.html; and "Civility is now a foreign concept in Americans politics. How did we get here—and how we fix it?" https://www.nbcnews.com/think/opinion/civility-now-foreign-concept-americans-politics-how-did-we-get-ncna873491.

11. https://www.npr.org/2021/03/19/977879589/yes-capitol-rioters-were-armed-here-are-the-weapons-prosecutors-say-they-used.

12. https://www.washingtonpost.com/politics/2021/05/18/clyde-tourist-capitol-riot-photos/.

He has downplayed the violence of that day, calling it "forgettably minor." He has also described those events as mere "vandalism."

It is almost as if the Marvel Cinematic Universe's notion of a multiverse is unfolding before our eyes[13]

Of greater concern are the many challenges to longstanding legal norms, especially with regards to elections. State after state is overturning or rewriting the laws that govern who can vote, as well as when and where individuals can vote. Proponents argue that these changes are necessary to ensure fair and untainted election results. Cynics argue that these proposed laws are merely means to suppress voter turnout among young people and people of color.

The legal fights over mask mandates and vaccine requirements are more troubling and too numerous to delineate.

The question is, are these real threats to the legal systems of either country? Can the law and thus freedom be sustained in the face of such prolonged attacks? Here we turn again to the Exodus narrative for some answers, comfort, and even perhaps some reason to be optimistic.

As we have pointed out throughout this book, the Exodus saga did not end when the Jews triumphantly left Egypt. It did not end when they arrived at Mount Sinai and accepted God's laws upon themselves. Instead, this story reaches its true conclusion only when the Jewish people arrived at the land God had promised their forefathers. Arrival in the promised land took forty long years. They were contentious years, too. The Torah itself testifies to this, as God tells Moses that the Jewish people "tried Me these many (Lit. "ten") times and have disobeyed Me."[14] There were people who wanted a different god and a different leader. There were others who advocated for going back to Egypt. Things were so bad that God was tempted—on more than one occasion—to destroy

---

13. For readers who have somehow managed to escape the Disney/Marvel onslaught, here is the simplest definition of the multiverse concept. The multiverse is infinite. Vastly different parallel worlds, along with vastly different realms of existence, all exist. Anything and everything can happen with them.

14. Numbers 14:22. The Talmud (Erchin 15a) enumerates the specifics of each of these ten trials.

the Jewish people, but He allowed Himself to be dissuaded by the impassioned pleas of Moses on behalf of them.[15]

Compared to this, perhaps things are not quite as bad in the United States as they sometimes seem.

In all seriousness, this is an essential part of the enduring lesson of the Exodus story. Exodus is meant to teach that freedom is a prerequisite for one to commit to following the law. That is the "leave Egypt and go to Mount Sinai" part of the story. The "wandering in the wilderness" part of the story reminds us that vocal and even sometimes violent minorities can create challenges for a society that seeks freedom and desires to undergird it with law. Taken together, these two parts teach that freedom requires law, and that substantive law is only sustainable within the context of freedom. This is the true essence of *halakha*, just as it is the true essence of what America's founders envisioned for the country they were birthing.

The Exodus story ends with a cliffhanger. The final chapters of the Torah tell us that the Jewish people are poised to enter the holy land. In the face of his impending death, Moses appoints a new leader, Joshua, to take the people across the Jordan River and to conquer the land. Yet the Torah ends with the death of Moses, not the Jewish people conquering and settling the land of Canaan. Will the people succeed in this quest? The book of Joshua tells us that they do.[16] Of that there was no doubt. That is not why the Torah abruptly ends the Exodus story, leaving it incomplete. Instead, perhaps, the Torah is imparting one final lesson: that the task of building a society that embraces freedom and safeguards it with the law is never done, and each generation has an obligation and a duty to further that task. Joshua understood this. So, too, did the

15. The incidents which led God to consider destroying the Jewish people include their worship of the Golden Calf (Exodus 32:1–14), the people's response to the report of the spies (Numbers 13:1–33), Korah's rebellion (Numbers 16:1–40), and their sinfully promiscuous behavior with the daughters of Moab (Numbers 25:1–9).

16. Whether archeological evidence comes to the same conclusion is a matter of debate. See, for example, Jennifer Wallace, "Shifting Ground in the Holy Land."

leaders who came after him. Some were more successful than others, as the Bible and history tell us. There were certainly times in Jewish history when both their leaders and the Jewish people lost sight of this. They compromised or abandoned the rule of law and subsequently lost the freedoms they desired. However, they never lost hope for its restoration as evidenced by the many prayers within Jewish liturgy calling for this.

America may be at a crossroads, but the ending of the Exodus story reminds us that with strong leaders and an equally strong commitment to the law, the promised land is always within reach. Challenges such as those we face today are but speed bumps on the road to the more perfect union envisioned by the Preamble to the United States Constitution.

CHAPTER SIX

Slavery in the Post-Exodus Jewish Legal Tradition and the Lessons It Offers America

W E HAVE, TO THIS POINT, shown how Exodus influenced America's founders and how those men and women intuited the key lesson of that story. That is, they understood that the freedom people seek via liberation can only be preserved if it is accompanied and sustained by a vibrant legal system.

There is one last interesting and, it must be said, ironic parallel between the American and Jewish legal systems that must be addressed. This parallel presents us with quite the conundrum.

America's founders railed against King George's oppressions. They delineated in the Declaration of Independence King George's "history of repeated injuries and usurpations, all having in direct object the establishment of an absolute Tyranny over these States" and then spent years fighting to free themselves from his oppressive rule. Indeed, the most famous words of the Declaration of Independence insist that "We hold these truths to be self-evident, that all men are created equal, that they are endowed by their Creator with certain unalienable Rights, that among these are Life, Liberty and the pursuit of Happiness." Yet, upon achieving their freedom and establishing their legal system, Americans failed to address or remedy the greatest oppression then present in the continental United States: slavery. It was if the phrase "all men" excluded black men. Worse still, they implicitly recognized slavery in the U.S. Constitution in two ways: with the infamous "three-fifths compromise"[1] and the Importation Clause.[2] Those who drafted and signed the Constitution seemingly sought to curtail slavery by banning the importation of slaves by 1808.[3] However, America's founders refused to end slavery outright. Historians provide many diverse answers to why this was and point out that it was not until the outbreak of civil war that slavery began to end in the U.S. Still, the contradictory and hypocritical stance taken by America's founders vis-à-vis slavery stands in sharp contrast to their lofty statements made in their pursuit of independence.

A similar conundrum underlies the Jewish legal system following the Exodus. How is it that the same God who liberates the Jewish people from slavery subsequently begins the civil code He gives them with the laws of slavery?[4] Why would God free the Jews from Egyptian bondage only to immediately allow them to own slaves?

Before tackling this difficult question, it is worth thinking about why the Torah's civil code began with the laws of slavery. Surely there must have been more pressing issues. The great

1. This compromise between delegates from the Northern and the Southern states at the 1787 Constitutional Convention established that the slave population in the Southern states would be counted for determining direct taxation and representation in the House of Representatives, but not fully. One black slave would only be counted as three-fifths of a white person. Said differently and more bluntly, these delegates explicitly declared in the U.S. Constitution that a slave was less than fully human.

2. Article I, Section 9, in which the Congress could not ban the slave trade for 20 years.

3. This was achieved by The Act Prohibiting Importation of Slaves of 1807 (2 Stat. 426, enacted March 2, 1807). This federal law provided that no new slaves were permitted to be imported into the United States. It took effect on January 1, 1808, the earliest date permitted by the United States Constitution.

4. According to the Rabbinic tradition, the civil laws that begin in chapter twenty-one of Exodus were given to the Jewish people at Mount Sinai along with the Ten Commandments.

biblical commentator Rabbi Moses Nachmanides explains why it makes sense to start this civil code with the laws of slavery. The law requires that a Hebrew slave ought to be set free after seven years; moreover, according to Nachmanides, this has great symbolic importance. He wrote:

> God began the first ordinance with the subject of a Hebrew servant, because the liberation of the servant in the seventh year contains a remembrance of the departure from Egypt which is mentioned in the first commandment, just as He said on it, *And thou shalt remember that thou wast a bondman in the land of Egypt, and the Eternal thy God redeemed thee; therefore I command thee this thing today (Deuteronomy 15:15).* It also contains a remembrance of the creation, just as the Sabbath does, for the seventh year signals to a servant a complete rest from the work of his master, just as the seventh day of the week does.[5]

Other commentators suggest a more practical logic for beginning the Jewish civil code with the laws of slavery, saying:

> The reason why the Torah commences its list of social laws with this particular law is that the Israelites had recently been redeemed from slavery themselves, so that they had good reason to understand how important it is not to treat one of their own as they had been treated in Egypt. Even if an Israelite had committed a crime for which he had been sold, the maximum length of time he was allowed to have his freedom to choose his employer restricted was six years. Even during these six years, his master, who did not own him bodily even then, was not allowed to force him to perform menial tasks.[6]

With these insights in hand, let us now turn to the great paradox before us, the one that has God freeing the Jews from slavery but then allowing them to own slaves.

---

5. See Nachmanides on Exodus 21:2.
6. See Chizkuni on Exodus 21:2.

Jewish law, as set forth in the Torah and expounded by the Talmud, uses a single term, *eved* (עֶבֶד, from the Hebrew word "worker"), to define two distinct classes of what English language refers to as slaves. The first is *eved ivri*, a Hebrew slave, as the verse states, "When you acquire a Hebrew slave, that person shall serve six years—and shall go free in the seventh year, without payment."[7]

Thinking of an *eved ivri* as a slave is incorrect, even though the Hebrew word *eved* can be and often is translated as a "slave." Here's why:

In biblical times, a Jewish court could sentence an individual to serve as an *eved ivri* for one of two reasons. If an individual stole an item and, after being caught, lacked the financial means to repay the victim for his or her loss, the court could declare him an *eved ivri*. Alternatively, an individual who could not pay off a debt owed to another could be sentenced to serve as an *eved ivri*. In both cases, the more accurate translation of *eved ivri* is "Hebrew servant," because the individual is more correctly akin to an indentured servant than a slave.[8]

Further underscoring the fact that an *eved ivri* is not a slave are the laws that govern his treatment by his or her "owner." According to Torah law, an *eved ivri* is a full-fledged Jew in all respects. This individual is obligated in all the commandments of the Torah and is included in most respects as a member of the owner's family. An *eved ivri* may bring his own family, including wife and children, along with him as he works to repay his debt, and his "owner" is obligated to support his family as well as the *eved ivri* himself. The owner is obligated to treat the *eved ivri* so humanely that the Talmudic sages state, "anyone who acquires a Hebrew slave acquires a master for himself."[9] How so? "He must be with [i.e., equal to] you in food and drink, that you should not

7. Exodus 21:2.

8. It must be noted that later rabbis eliminated the category of *eved ivri*. Rabbi Shimon ben Tzemach Duran, the fourteenth-fifteenth century Spanish and North African authority known as the Tashbetz, ruled that this legal category ceased to exist after the exile of the ten northern tribes of Israel.

9. Kiddushin 20a.

eat white bread and he black bread, you drink old wine and he new wine, you sleep on a feather bed and he on straw." [10]

The second type of *eved* (עֶבֶד) discussed in the Torah aligns more closely with the image of a slave in the pre–Civil War southern states. Nonetheless, the Torah envisions slavery far differently than slave owners and state law in the antebellum South. That said, we must ultimately address the issue of why the Torah allows slavery at all.

The Torah defines its second type of slave in the book of Leviticus, which reads:

> Such male and female slaves as you may have—it is from the nations round about you that you may acquire male and female slaves. You may also buy them from among the children of alien residents among you, or from their families that are among you, whom they begot in your land. These shall become your property: you may keep them as a possession for your children after you, for them to inherit as property for all time. Such you may treat as slaves. But as for your Israelite kin, no one shall rule ruthlessly over another. [11]

This passage seems eerily familiar. Were not the Jews in Egypt treated "as property for all time," they and their children alike? How can this be? Why would God allow this?

It is important to remember that Jewish law is based on both the written text (Torah) and the oral tradition (Talmud). Only by consulting both can one understand and appreciate the true meaning of any given law. When it comes to slavery, the oral tradition has much to add. Indeed, it fundamentally changes the status and circumstances of foreign-born slaves that Jews may possess.

Let's start with the notion of ownership. The Talmudic sages make clear that one does not have any true ownership rights over a slave. When a Jew acquires a foreign-born slave, he or she merely acquires the rights to the slave's labor. The Talmud states:

10. Kiddushin 20a.
11. Leviticus 25:44–46.

> His previous **gentile** owner **did not have ownership of the** slave's **body,** since a gentile is unable to have ownership of another's body; rather, he had rights to only the slave's labor. And only **that which he owned in him was he** able to **sell to** the Jew. [emphasis added][12]

The implications of this limitation should be obvious. As the Torah makes clear, a Jewish slave owner is not free to do as he or she wishes with the foreign-born slave. Here then is the first difference in the Torah's concept of slavery: all slaves—whether Jewish or not—had basic human rights, including the right not to be killed and/or beaten. Slaves were people in the Jewish tradition, albeit that they were not free to work anywhere they wished.

In the ancient world, slaves were considered to be and were treated like animals.[13] Not so in Torah law, where the life of a slave "is not the property of the master, but rather of the One Who gives all life—and it is He Who demands his blood from the hands of those who spill it—whether this be the master or someone else."[14] Similarly, one may not "rule over them ruthlessly,"[15] nor may one treat them badly.[16] A master may chastise a slave to a reasonable extent[17] but not wound him. If one were to cause bodily harm to his or her slave, the slave would go free.[18] The prohibition to murder applied to one's slave.

This position stands in contrast to the situation in pre-Civil War United States, where killing one's slave was never construed as

12. Yevamot 46a. By way of comparison, consider the infamous Dred Scott of 1857 in which the U.S. Supreme court ruled that slaves were property under the Fifth Amendment and that any law that would deprive a slave owner of that property was unconstitutional.

13. This was often and predominantly how slaves were viewed in the antebellum South.

14. Rav Elchanan Samet, Mishpatim/Slavery, https://etzion.org.il/en/tanakh/torah/sefer-shemot/parashat-mishpatim/mishpatim-slavery.

15. Leviticus 25:43.

16. Leviticus 25:40.

17. Ecclesiasticus 33:26.

18. Exodus 21:26–27.

murder in many of the places where slavery was legal. [19] We thus see a second difference in the Torah's understanding of slavery: slaves in the Jewish tradition are owned people, not property with no human rights.

Further differences abound. Jewish law places limits on the work one may demand of a foreign-born slave. The workload of a slave should never exceed his physical strength,[20] nor should a slave be given pointless, mind-numbing tasks, such as digging a deep hole only to immediately refill it.[21] The slave could not be made to work on the Jewish Sabbath and even had the status of a partial Jew, requiring that he be circumcised and immersed in a pool as part of a quasi-conversion ritual. He was even given kosher food to eat and was obligated by much of Jewish law. Perhaps most important of all, a fugitive slave must not be turned over to his master but rather given refuge.[22]

There is a final point about foreign-born slaves that makes this Talmudic perspective on slave ownership clear. There is a lengthy debate among the Sages about whether it is permissible for a Jew to own a non-circumcised male slave. The most extreme position is that of Rabbi Akiva, who maintains that one may not keep an uncircumcised slave even for a moment.[23] At its core, this dispute reflects the rabbinic concern about having idolatrous influences in one's household. Once the slave is circumcised, the slave is required to abandon any previous idolatrous practices he formally had and instead must keep the same commandments of a

19. For more on this, see Andrew T. Fede, *Homicide Justified*.

20. Ecclesiasticus 33:28–29.

21. In his legal code (Mishneh Torah, Laws of Slaves 9:8), Maimonides clarifies this point: "It is permissible to have a Canaanite slave perform excruciating labor (pharekh). Although this is the law, the attribute of piety and the ways of wisdom is for a person to be compassionate and to pursue justice, not to excessively burden his slaves, nor cause them distress."

22. Deuteronomy 23:16. Again by way of comparison, consider The Fugitive Slave Act of 1850. The act required that slaves be returned to their owners, even if they were in a free state. The act also made the federal government responsible for finding, returning, and trying escaped slaves.

23. Yevamot 48b.

free woman. This makes a slave closer to a Jew than a *ger toshav* (a "righteous Gentile" who must keep only the seven Noahide laws[24]). This is presumably a precursor to fully accepting the Jewish faith. Should the slave ultimately opt not to become fully Jewish, he must be freed at the end of twelve months.

Become one of us or leave. Hard to imagine a stronger anti-slavery attitude.

To be clear, we do not offer up these caveats and limitations as apologies for the slavery of the Torah. Even if Jewish ownership was better than their prior circumstances (or better than enslaved people in the antebellum South), foreign-born slaves in the possession of Jews were still slaves and thus not free. This still leaves us to answer the question of why God allowed this practice.

Jewish scholars, both ancient and modern, have wrestled with this question. They offer a variety of answers. Below are the ones we find most poignant and compelling.

A defining tenet of Judaism is how it understands God's relationship with humankind. God made a covenant with the Jewish people and designated them as His "chosen nation." The why's and how's of this are beyond the scope of this discussion. Suffice to say that the mission of the Jewish people is to be "a light to the nations."[25] However, humankind is expected to believe in and worship the one, true God.

Here is how this idea of covenant relates to slavery.

When God revealed Himself to the Jewish people at Mount Sinai, slavery was universally accepted among the nations. God could have banned slavery among the Jews, but it would still have been prevalent, with all its violence and inhumanity, among Israel's neighbors. It thus follows for Jewish scholars that when God allows Jews to own slaves, it was meant to temper the institution

24. The Noahide laws consist of the following: do not worship idols; do not curse God; do not murder; do not commit adultery or sexual immorality; do not steal; do not eat flesh torn from a living animal; and establish courts of justice.

25. Isaiah 60:3.

and improve the lot of slaves. As Rabbi Sampson Rafael Hirsch—
the great nineteenth century Jewish Scholar—described it:

> The consideration of certain circumstances is necessary,
> correctly to understand the fact that the Torah presup-
> poses and allows the possession and purchase of slaves
> from abroad to a nation itself just released from slavery.
> No Jew could make any other human being into a slave.
> He could only acquire by purchase, people who, by the
> then universally accepted international law, were already
> slaves. But his transference into the property of a Jew was
> the one and only salvation for anybody who, according
> to the prevailing laws of the nations, was stamped as a
> slave. The terribly sad experiences of the last century[26]
> teach us how completely unprotected and liable to the
> most inhuman treatment was the slave who in accor-
> dance with the national law was not emancipated, and
> even when emancipated, where he was, looked upon as
> still belonging to the slave class, or as a freed-slave. The
> home of a Jew was to them a home of freedom.[27]

Per this view, slavery was allowed (but not encouraged) in
Jewish law as a way to improve the lot of slaves and grant them
certain basic rights that they would not have otherwise enjoyed.

A corollary of this approach is that the Jewish institution of
slavery was meant as a countermeasure to the barbarism of that
institution generally. In a sense, the rationale for allowing Jews to
own slaves was to make society more moral. Admittedly, this sort
of morality was less than ideal. It may have been true that the Jewish model of slavery was predicated on slaves being human, but the
common model of that time allowed enslaved people to be dehu-
manized. Given this, how was this Jewish model more "moral?" It
turned slavery into a form of forced proselytization (even though
Judaism in general is against proselytizing) by demanding that
foreign-born slaves abandon their idolatrous ways.

---

26. Rabbi Hirsch's commentary on the Torah (*Uebersetzung und Erk-
lärung des Pentateuchs*) was published between 1867 and 1878.

27. Rabbi S.R. Hirsch commentary on Exodus 12:44.

In this final chapter, we have posed several difficult questions, and we believe it necessary to ask one more. Given the depravations and inhumanity of slavery, how could either legal tradition—American or Jewish—have countenanced a slow and gradual approach to abolishing it?

Of America's first twelve presidents, only John Adams and his son John Quincy Adams, were non-slave holders.[28] The elder Adams was known for his opposition to slavery but did not support abolitionism except if it was done in a "gradual" way with "much caution and Circumspection." Adams also dismissed radical abolitionist measures as "produc[ing] greater violations of Justice and Humanity, than the continuance of the practice" of slavery itself.[29]

Even the great emancipator himself, Abraham Lincoln, hoped the southern states might adopt "systems of gradual emancipation." In general, he thought the best path toward eliminating slavery had to include "three main features—gradual [emancipation]—compensation—and vote of the people." These requirements, he admitted, would make for a slow process, but slowness might have the benefit of allowing the "two races" to "gradually live themselves out of their old relation to each other, and both come out better prepared for the new."[30]

We Americans know first-hand how difficult it was to uproot slavery, despite its evils and depravations, given that it undergirded America's economy in so many ways and for so many years. It took a devastating and bloody civil war to finally have slavery declared illegal, and it took another 100 years for legislation to be passed by Congress to grant African-American citizens the rights they thought had been bestowed upon them with the passage of the Thirteenth, Fourteenth, and Fifteenth Amendments.[31]

28. https://www.statista.com/statistics/1121963/slaves-owned-by-us-presidents/.

29. "John Adams on the abolition of slavery, 1801," https://www.gilderlehrman.org/history-resources/spotlight-primary-source/john-adams-abolition-slavery-1801.

30. Abraham Lincoln and Emancipation, https://billofrightsinstitute.org/essays/abraham-lincoln-and-emancipation.

31. The Thirteenth Amendment, ratified in 1865, ended slavery. The

Why America did not end slavery earlier or why America allowed the freed slaves to be virtually re-enslaved in the decades after the Civil War is a contentious and much-debated topic.[32] We see it reflected in debates about Critical Race Theory and whether it is or ought to be taught in schools. We hear it in arguments about systemic racism and whether and how it continues to impact American society.

We have no answers to such questions other than to say that it seems obvious to us that while the passage of the Thirteenth Amendment may have formally ended slavery in the United States, we as a country still feel the aftereffects of slavery. Nonetheless, we think it helpful to turn once again to the Exodus narrative for some perspective.

As we have pointed out, God opted to give humankind seven basic laws even though the Jewish people were given 613 commandments.[33] Having thus decided not to end slavery among the nations by Divine edict, God gave specific and detailed laws to the Jewish people regarding this institution. We think God did so for several reasons, first and foremost, to teach us that there are some societal problems that cannot be solved quickly or easily by law. What law can do is lessen a bad situation until society musters the will and means to fully tackle the problem. This approach also demonstrates the idea that additional and future regulation is worthwhile and can be used to further ameliorate the situation.

This is perhaps what drove America's founders to implicitly recognize slavery (via the "three-fifths compromise") rather than

---

Fourteenth Amendment, ratified in 1868, granted the former slaves full citizenship rights, and the Fifteenth Amendment, ratified in 1870, prohibits the denial of the right to vote based on race, color or previous condition of servitude.

32. For more on this, see Douglas A. Blackman, Slavery by Another Name.

33. The tradition of the Jewish people being given *taryag* (that is, 613) commandments mitzvot was advanced by Rabbi Simlai of the Talmud. He reasoned as follows: Scripture relates that Moses commanded the Torah to the Jewish people. The numerical equivalent of the four Hebrew letters of the word *Torah* is 611. By adding to this the two commandments which all the Jews heard from God Himself at Mount Sinai, we arrive at a total of 613.

completely ignore the status quo. This, too, could explain the Constitution's eventual ban on the future import of slaves. It was a small step intended to make the evils of slavery somehow less evil.

The Jewish legal tradition embraces the idea of using law to make bad situations better even if it does not fully resolve the problem. Rabbi Nachum Rabinovitch gave us an interesting perspective on this. He once noted that the Torah "encompasses legislation and commands to combat the forces of evil and destruction that erupt within the individual's soul and the nation's spirit and to ensure that the necessary conditions for spiritual development are satisfied to the greatest possible extent, given each generation's situation and the social, economic, and cultural circumstances prevalent at any given time and place."[34]

Rabbi Rabinovitch's approach seems an apt one for the Torah's laws of slavery. It took the Jewish people centuries to finally walk away from slavery, even though it was clear from the biblical narrative and Talmudic sources that slavery was seen as undesirable. Rabbi Jonathan Sacks famously put this into perspective: "Slavery, like vengeance, is a vicious circle that has no natural end. Why not, then, give it a supernatural end? Why did God not say: There shall be no more slavery?"[35] He went on to give a profound answer, saying:

> Change is possible in human nature but it takes time: time on a vast scale, centuries, even millennia. There is little doubt that in terms of the Torah's value system the exercise of power by one person over another, without their consent, is a fundamental assault against human dignity. This is not just true of the relationship between master and slave. It is even true, according to many classic Jewish commentators, of the relationship between king and subjects, rulers and ruled. According to the Sages it is even true of the relationship between God and human beings.

34. Nahum Eliezer Rabinovitch, "The Way of Torah."

35. "The Slow End of Slavery," https://www.rabbisacks.org/covenant-conver sation/mishpatim/the-slow-end-of-slavery/.

In God's ideal world, the one we are tasked with creating, there would be no slavery. Yet, it is a fundamental principle of God's relationship with humankind that He does not force us to change faster than we are able to do so of our own free will. Thus, the Torah does not abolish slavery but instead sets in motion a series of fundamental laws that will lead people, albeit at their own pace, to abolish slavery. In other words, God does not abolish slavery outright. He instead begins the Jewish civil code with a law intended to make a bad situation incrementally better, as the verse states, "that person shall serve six years—and shall go free in the seventh year, without payment."

Would America and the Jewish people be different had we not opted for incrementalism but had instead been able to abolish slavery much faster? Certainly, but recognizing the struggles involved in ending slavery allows us to see the growth and progress both peoples—American and Jewish—have made in building better and more moral societies. It is possible that the discomfort and shame we feel for allowing slavery to exist as long as it did will continue to motivate us to work harder and faster when we face other morally challenging circumstances.

The notion of wrestling with the morally challenging parts of our lives and our society brings us back to the core thesis in this book.

Remember that God's charge to the Jewish people at Sinai was to be "a kingdom of priests and a holy nation."[36] Nowhere is freedom found in this exhortation even though the Jews had been freed from slavery only seven weeks prior. That is because, as we have argued, the Jews were not liberated merely to become a free people. God wanted them and expected them to evolve into a nation committed to creating a law-abiding society. From this perspective, freedom is a necessary precondition to achieving its goal.

America's founders understood this and wove this idea into the basic fabric of the democracy they were creating. What has for centuries set America apart from other nations is its synergistic

36. Exodus 19:5–6.

linking between freedom and the law, which, of course, is something that goes to the heart of the Exodus story.

The first of the national goals enumerated in the Preamble to the US Constitution is "to form a more perfect Union," followed by "to establish Justice." We truly believe that America is and always has been a great country, so much so that we have never fully understood the "Make America Great Again" mantra. Yet, greatness does not equate to perfection, and America's history is marked by episodes, slavery foremost among them, that were far from the founder's stated goals for their emerging nation.

Falling short of the mark, as the American and Jewish people have done more times than either would like to remember, does not negate their aspirational national goals. It simply means that we must be prepared to honestly assess morally challenging situations when they arise and then recommit ourselves to our goals, be it becoming "a kingdom of priests and a holy nation" or creating "a more perfect Union."

Never losing sight of this is the true enduring lesson of Exodus.

Bibliography

Arraf, Jan. "15 Years After U.S. Invasion, Some Iraqis Are Nostalgic For Saddam Hussein Era." *Parallels*. April 30, 2018. https://www.npr.org/sections/paral lels/2018/04/30/605240844/15-years-after-u-s-invasion-some-iraqis-are-nostalgic-for-saddam-hussein-era.

Berkowitz, Peter. The Court, the Constitution, and the Culture of Freedom: Abortion, affirmative action, and same-sex marriage." Hoover Institution. https://www.hoover.org/research/court-constitution-and-culture-freedom.

Besdin, Rabbi Abraham. *Reflections of the Rav: Lessons in Jewish Thought.* New York: KTAV Publishing House, 1993 [orig. 1979].

Blackman, Douglas A. Slavery by Another Name: The Re-Enslavement of Black Americans from the Civil War to World War II. New York: Anchor Books. 2008.

Brooks, David. Globalization Is Over. The Global Culture Wars Have Begun," *New York Times*, April 8, 2022, https://www.nytimes.com/2022/04/08/opinion/globalization-global-culture-war.html?referringSource=articleS hare.

Broyde, Michael J. "What Does Jewish Law Think American Abortion Law Ought To Be?" https://thelehrhaus.com/timely-thoughts/what-does-jewish-law-think-american-abortion-law-ought-to-be/.

Elazar, Daniel J. "The Book of Joshua as a Political Classic." Jerusalem Center for Public Affairs. https://www.jcpa.org/dje/articles2/joshua.htm.

Ellis, Joseph J. The Quartet: Orchestrating the Second American Revolution, *1783-1789*. New York: Alfred A. Knopf, 2015.

Farber, Dr. Rabbi Zev "Does the Torah Really Want Us to Appoint a King?" TheTorah.com. https://www.thetorah.com/article/does-the-torah-really-want-us-to-appoint-a-king.

Fede, Andrew T. *Homicide Justified: The Legality of Killing Slaves in the United States and the Atlantic World.* Athens. University of Georgia Press, 2017.

Feiler, Bruce. *America's Prophet: How the Story of Moses Shaped America.* New York: Harper Collins, 2009.

Bibliography

Feldman, Rabbi Emanuel. "The Odd and Instructive Habits of Non-Observant Jews: A Look at Berit Milah and Pesah." *Tradition: A Journal of Orthodox Jewish Thought* 41, no. 2 (2008): 127–37.

Fodiman-Silverman, Ilana. "Salvation from servitude: A Passover tale of the midrash." *The Jerusalem Post*. April 26, 2019.

Foner, Eric. *The Story of American Freedom*. New York: W.W. Norton & Company, 1998.

Freund, Michael. "How the Exodus Story Created America." *Jerusalem Post*. March 29, 2013. https://www.jpost.com/opinion/columnists/how-the-exodus-story-created-america-308136.

Goldstone, Jack A. *Revolutions: A Very Short Introduction*. Oxford: Oxford University Press, 2014.

Hawn, C. Michael. "History of Hymns: 'Go Down, Moses.'" Discipleship Ministries. March 13, 2019. https://www.umcdiscipleship.org/resources/history-of-hymns-go-down-moses.

Henrich, Joseph. *The WEIRDest People in the World*. New York: Farrar, Straus and Giroux, 2020.

Jakobovits, Immanuel. *The Timely and the Timeless: Jews, Judaism and Society in a Storm-tossed Decade*. London: Vallentine Mitchel Publishers, 1977.

Maume, Chris. "It was better to live in Iraq under Saddam." *Independent*. June 12, 2014. https://www.independent.co.uk/voices/comment/it-was-better-live-iraq-under-saddam-9532742.html.

Mikkelson, David. "Mussolini and On Time Trains. Did Mussolini make the trains run on time?" Snopes.com. https://www.snopes.com/fact-check/loco-motive/.

Novak, David. "Universal Moral Law in the Theology of Hermann Cohen." *Modern Judaism* 1, no. 1 (1981): 101–17.

Rabinovitch, Nahum Eliezer. "The Way of Torah," *Edah Journal* 3, no. 1 (*Tevet* 5763).

Roberts, Cokie. *Founding Mothers: The Women Who Raised Our Nation*. New York: Harper Perennial, 2005.

Sacks, Rabbi Jonathan. "The Birth of a New Freedom." https://rabbisacks.org/covenant-conversation-5772-ki-tissa-the-birth-of-a-new-freedom/.

Schlesinger, Jr., Arthur. *The Imperial Presidency*. New York: Mariner Books, 2004 [orig. 1973].

Tanakh: A New Translation of the Holy Scriptures according to the Traditional Hebrew Text. Philadelphia: Jewish Publication Society, 1985.

Tiruneh, Gizachew. "Social Revolutions: Their Causes, Patterns, and Phases." SAGE Open. July-September 2014: 1–12.10.1177/2158244014548845.

Wallace, Jennifer. "Shifting Ground in the Holy Land." *Smithsonian Magazine*. https://www.smithsonianmag.com/history/shifting-ground-in-the-holy-land-114897288/.

Zuckerman, Phil and Andrew Seidel. "The Supreme Court's right-wing Catholics are destroying true religious freedom." September 14, 2021, Salon.com.

Bibliography

https://www.salon.com/2021/09/14/the-supreme-courts-right-wing
-catholics-are-destroying-true-religious-freedom/.